GREEN G

Allotment
Gardening

This is a **FLAME TREE** book
First published in 2010

Publisher and Creative Director: Nick Wells
Project Editor: Catherine Taylor
Art Director: Mike Spender
Layout Design: Dave Jones
Digital Design and Production: Chris Herbert
Picture Research: Polly Prior, Catherine Taylor and Chelsea Edwards
Proofreader: Dawn Laker
Indexer: Helen Snaith

To Naomi Goddard

Special thanks to: Polly Prior, Chelsea Edwards and William Greaves

10 12 14 13 11
1 3 5 7 9 10 8 6 4 2

This edition first published 2010 by
FLAME TREE PUBLISHING
Crabtree Hall, Crabtree Lane
Fulham, London SW6 6TY
United Kingdom

www.flametreepublishing.com

Flame Tree Publishing is part of The Foundry Creative Media Co. Ltd

ISBN 978-1-84786-696-7

A CIP record for this book is available from the British Library upon request.

The author has made all reasonable efforts to ensure that the information in this book is correct at the time of
going to print, and the publishers cannot accept any liability for incorrect or out-of-date information.
The publisher would be glad to rectify any omissions in future editions of this book.

Printed in China

Thanks to **HAXNICKS** for supplying the images on pages 118, 143, 141t – www.haxnicks.co.uk, 0845 241 1555.
The images on pages 175, 177 © Rasbak*; 176 © Jeff Kubina; 180b © Sten Porse*. The image on page 198b is courtesy of iStock and © Sebastien Cote.
All remaining images are courtesy of Shutterstock and © the following photographers: 1 & 83 Pontus Edenberg; 3 & 4b & 39, 62, 75 Jerome Whittingham;
4t Ttphoto; 5b & 121 Foxy; 5c & 106 Neil Webster; 5t & 70 Victor I. Makhankov; 6b & 170b Andy Poole; 6b & 216 Ale‰ Studeń; 6t & 146 Boris Khamitsevich;
7t & 193t Alex Kuzovlev; 8, 91, 141b forestpath; 9 Jaimie Duplass; 11, 101 Ed Phillips; 12 Alex Hinds; 15 Nicholas Sutcliffe; 17 Fotokostic; 20 Florin C; 22 Sandra van
der Steen; 24 jeff gynane; 26 Christopher Elwell; 28, 78 InavanHateran; 32, 34 Timothy Large; 37, 116, 136, 152, 192b, 207 Denis & Yulia Pogostins; 38 Emily
Veinglory; 42 Mark William Richardson; 44 Vasily Mulyukin; 45, 125 Stephen Aaron Rees; 47 Brendan Howard; 50 Danie Nel; 52 tonobalaguerf; 53 sharon kingston;
54, 71 hairy mallow; 56 Elnur; 57 jocrebbin; 58 N. Mitchell; 60 Pavelk; 64 Kate Bross; 65 Stefan Fierros; 66 Aleksandar Todorovic; 68 Zubareva Maria; 71 Westbury;
72 Olga Lipatova; 74 IgorGolovniov; 77 Amy Johansson; 80 Jenny Horne; 82 GSPhotography; 84b spfotocz; 84c Simon Krzic; 84t iwka; 85b Margo Harrison; 85t, 202
Sally Wallis; 86b Dole; 86c Danny Smythe; 86t Pakimon; 87 Mike Flippo; 88 Pefkos; 89 Lucy Baldwin; 90, 98 Pack Shot; 92 Vince Clements; 93 Georgy Markov; 95b
mehmetcan; 95t, 110, 195b LianeM; 97 slowfish; 100 Alexey Chernitevich; 104, 111 DanielYordanov; 105 Rosinka; 108 Norma Cornes; 109 Michaela Steininger;
114 Christina Richards; 122 Ioana Drutu; 123 accesslab; 126 Kevin Lepp; 127 Elena Elisseeva; 129 Anthony Harris; 131 El Greco; 132 Adisa; 134 Darren Hester;
138 LILIYA777; 139 Polina Lobanova; 145 Sofia; 148, 166 Stefan Fierros; 151b Scott Rothstein; 151t ericlefrancais; 155 italianestro; 156 Sergej Razvodovskij;
159t Charles B. Ming Onn; 159b Kenneth V. Pilon; 161, 219 xtrekx; 162 ason; 163 Tish1; 164 artproem; 168 Michael Pettigrew; 170t Val Thoermer; 171 Jean Frooms;
172 Goydenko Tatiana; 173 Filipe B. Varela; 178 NicolasMcComber; 180t, 182, 183 Sergey Chushkin; 184 sevenke; 185 Damian Herde; 187 Kris Butler; 189, 236
ukrphoto; 190 Vladislav Gajic; 191 Branislav Senic; 192t Lynn Whitt; 193b kiya-nochka; 194 Monika Gniot; 195t Carmen Brunner; 197 Tobik; 198t marilyn barbone;
200 Dianne McFadden; 201 LUCARELLI TEMISTOCLE; 203 Studio 1a Photography; 204 Susan Montgomery; 205 Terry Reimink; 206b David Hughes; 206t Andrew
Chin; 209 A.Kozyreva; 210 LockStockBob; 212 Brzostowska; 213 Kruglov_Orda; 214 robert paul van beets; 215 Stefanie Mohr Photography; 217 Iain Frazer;
218 Roonie_70; 221 Simon@naffarts.co.uk; 222 Sharon Day; 224b X-etra; 224t Michael Ansell Photography; 226 Mona Makela; 226 Robert Redelowski;
227 DUSAN ZIDAR; 229 Adam Lu; 230 SerrNovik; 231 Denton Rumsey; 232 Dancing Fish; 233 Sally Graham; 234 erkanupan; 235 Ingrid Balabanova; 237 Lepas;
238 Nathalie Dulex; 241 Olga Utlyakova; 242 Michael C. Gray; 244 OlgaLis; 245 AGITA; 252 yalayama
*Used under the following licenses: http://creativecommons.org/licenses/by-sa/3.0/; http://en.wikipedia.org/wiki/GNU_Free_Documentation_License

GREEN GUIDES
Allotment Gardening

JEZ ABBOTT

Foreword by LUCY HALSALL,
editor of *Grow Your Own* magazine

FLAME TREE
PUBLISHING

Contents

Allotments bring happiness for all sorts of reasons, from encouraging healthy lifestyles to teaching you about food and how to grow your own. They help people with little or no gardens to get back to nature and tap into crucial topics like wildlife, biodiversity and sustainability. They also form teeming social hubs in the community, places to meet like-minded people, have fun and swap everything from fruit and vegetables to gossip.

Wherever you live, allotments are never far, but securing one for you and your family takes a little effort. Sites are often tucked away behind terraced houses or along canals, and you need to know what makes a good allotment for you and who to approach. A few handy hints never go amiss and this chapter tells you all you need to fast-track your application and fulfil your dream of making that allotment yours.

Planning Your Plot 48

The fun starts here: you've secured your plot but how can you tame that land and make it a productive powerhouse brimming with all the fruit, vegetables and flowers you want? You need to know how much space you require and how to decide what food to grow. Meanwhile, the questions you on have on soil, crops and how to lay out your plot will all be answered on these pages.

Preparing to Garden 80

This chapter looks at all the tools and equipment you will need and how to go about clearing your plot. Before long you will want to know about compost, seeds and plants and how to go about improving your soil, enriching it and then digging it to achieve the best results.

Gardening Time 112

When and how should you sow your seeds, how do you protect your tender young plants and how much should you water them? Working on the allotment is a constant learning curve, made easier by this chapter, which fills you in on all you need to know on organic plots, how often to visit your site and what to do if your busy working life rules out prolonged regular visits.

Harvesting Fruit and Vegetables

Harvest time will be busy and rewarding as you
reach peak performance on the plot. Now you need
to glean all the facts on when to harvest your fruit,
vegetables and flowers, how to go about harvesting
and how to store your bounty. A productive
allotment yields a staggering amount of produce
and you will want to know about freezing, drying
and canning all that delicious food.

Troubleshooting

No allotment is without a few
problems and this chapter is a
must-read for those who want to
know more about plant pests,
diseases and weeds. What
exactly is that unruly thatch in
the corner of your plot and how
can you blitz those caterpillars
and aphids? You need all your
wits to beat these tenacious
foes, and our expert guidance is
the perfect ally to give you the
start you need.

Fruit and Flowers 186

Want to know what to grow on your plot? This chapter tells you just that, and you will be amazed. Allotments flourish with an abundance of fruit trees, berries, currant bushes and a few exotic delights such as delicious grapes. Yes, you can grow them, along with beautiful flowers for the vase and a host of plants that look good, smell wonderful and help deter unwelcome pests such as aphids.

Vegetables and Herbs 208

Many vegetables go back thousands of years but the latest generations are right there on your plot. Enjoying them as much as the ancient Egyptians or Romans did, however, calls for know-how on when to plant and how to grow and harvest fresh food. You choice of vegetables and herbs is delightfully mind-boggling and flicking through this chapter will give a taste of what is in store for you and your family. Prepare to meet the burgeoning onion and cabbage families, the beans, the peas, the root vegetables, the beautiful tender aubergines and the allotment aristocrats, asparagus and globe artichoke.

Foreword

The desire to have an allotment plot is one felt by many more people than before, thanks to the grow-your-own revolution. Many gardeners have already discovered this rewarding method of producing food, and the passion is infectious – for those of us new to the venture, the urge to grab a spade and get started is a strong one.

There are a huge number of incentives for finding a plot. It's an obvious choice for people without a garden of any kind, or perhaps you need more growing space. You may want to grow crops organically, to cut down on food bills or simply yearn to try exciting new crops that supermarket shelves simply don't stock. One thing is for certain – 'food miles' will be a phrase of the past for you!

Once you rent your allotment you'll experience numerous immediate benefits: you'll get a great form of exercise, meet and make friends with other members of your community, exchange tips and successes with your neighbouring allotment holders and, ultimately, be eating delicious fruit and veg that you've grown yourself at its peak of freshness.

To get the most out of your plot, it pays to have a good knowledge of the potential it has to offer, and this is where *Allotment Gardening* is invaluable. It's an essential read for anyone new to 'allotmenting', and author Jez Abbott provides indispensable advice throughout the book on key areas, including how to

enhance your success on a waiting list, clear a neglected allotment, maximize your time on the plot and create a successful cropping plan to ensure your kitchen is bursting with wonderfully fresh produce year-round.

But of course, it's not just about visiting your plot – you need guidance on what to do when you're there and *Allotment Gardening* is packed with authoritative information on this too. So, whether you're a keen consumer of potatoes, carrots, salad leaves, tomatoes, chillies, spinach or strawberries, you'll find all the practical advice on how to sow, grow, harvest and preserve your favourite crop. And once you've got to grips with the basics, why not branch out into more diverse growing plans? Allotments can provide you with ample space to cultivate cut flowers, herbs, plants beneficial to wildlife and health-giving fruits such as goji berries and blueberries. It's not just about veg!

Over the next 200-plus pages, you'll find information that you can continually rely upon to ensure success on your allotment. It's certain that once well-thumbed, *Allotment Gardening* will arm you with sound knowledge to walk on to your plot with confidence.

Have a wonderfully productive time!

Lucy Halsall
EDITOR, *Grow Your Own* magazine

Introduction

The outdoors are back in again, which is great if you want to grow your own delicious and healthy food, meet like-minded gardeners and escape the humdrum office. Allotments tap into virtually all aspects of environmentalism and are perfect for people who want to take their food and health more seriously. Down on the allotment you are drawn to all walks of life from young professional women to old men in cloth caps, all transforming the dream of producing nutritious fruits and vegetables or gorgeous flowers into bountiful reality.

Am I Cut Out to be an Allotment Holder?

Anyone can be bitten by the allotment bug and today's tenant is far from the doddery but dated stereotype of an old codger with a whippet dog. Some grow grapevines, others pak choi. And while a few stalwarts still crave bigger leeks and ruder-shaped marrows, today's allotment holder is cosmopolitan and highly tuned to issues of climate and cultural diversity.

Why Have an Allotment?

An allotment may be the perfect answer to so many pressing concerns you have, such as:

- The rising cost of food and the additives used to enhance its look and flavour.
- 'Food miles', the distance food travels from where it is grown to the shop.
- Healthy eating and wanting your family to eat as much fresh food as possible.
- Meeting green-fingered people, making friends and doing more in the community.

Muck In

Until you have dug into your allotment it is hard to appreciate how much fresh produce will emerge from that same soil a few weeks later. A plastic punnet of fruit imported in darkest winter is no match for your strawberries, hand-picked at their ripest in balmy summer.

Digging Into the Past

The allotment bug is truly international and bites far and wide. Under Communism, plots were popular in Czechoslovakia, allotments grew in popularity during nineteenth-century industrialization in Germany, and allotments in Denmark date back to the 1770s. The golden age for allotments in England was between the wars, when imported foods were out and grow-your-own a must. But these parcels of land go way back to the Enclosure Acts of the 1700s, which gave unstoppable momentum to what became known as 'allotments'.

Tracts of land were let to the labouring poor and by the late 1800s were seen as an alternative to the workhouse. By the 1920s local authorities were obliged by law to provide allotments if there was demand. They were restricted to a maximum size of 40 poles, 1,000 sq m (1200 sq yards).

Hungry for War

The outbreak of the Great War saw demand soar as folks scrabbled to feed families, while the Second World War's great Dig for Victory was waged on 1.5 million plots. Interest waned in the 1960s, but a brief renaissance in the 1970s may owe a debt to popular UK TV comedy *The Good Life*.

Today's Toms, Barbaras and other converts to the good life are fighting for around 300,000 plots on 8,500 sites. Gardening is being hailed as a favourite pastime across Europe while interest in all things organic should ensure allotments endure well into the twenty-first century and beyond.

Did You Know?

Albert Einstein spent summers in the early 1920s in his allotment garden in Berlin-Spandau while other famous plot holders include the Queen of England.

Benefits

Working on an allotment takes time and can be tiring. But the paybacks are plentiful. Allotments steer you away from an increasingly work-oriented society, keep you physically fit and can improve your mental wellbeing. And of course allotments put food on your table.

Even if you are lucky enough to have a big garden it can rarely take the place of an allotment. The demand for a garden to be a grassed play area for children or an alfresco adornment to the home often rules out the serious business of growing copious amounts of fresh produce.

Allotments Stand Alone

This is where the allotment comes into its own, with all you need often near to hand. Advice from fellow allotment holders is never far away, and the make-do-and-mend mantra of this eco-community is very topical to all that's recyclable, sustainable and healthy.

The Allotment Ethos

Health is important, and hardly a day goes by without a horror story in the newspapers about fragmented society and 'broken Britain'. Working on an allotment gives you the chance to create a small community with bonds forged by a shared interest and a sharing culture. Allotments are social magnets, often drawing together people as diverse as the patchworks of land they tend. Here you will find bank managers and media types taking earnest advice on composting and crop rotation from a building labourer or nurse a few plots away.

Flexibility

The diverse nature of looking after an allotment reflects the varied nature of twenty-first century living. Not only can children, students and adults muck in, but you are not restricted to plots close to home. Some apply for allotments near work or close to their children's school.

Sustainability

Growing on allotments is one of the most sustainable activities you can undertake. If it's not eaten, produce is composted. Water run-off from sheds flows into a butt to irrigate the plants and virtually nothing ends up in landfill. Recycling is second nature to plot holders.

They think nothing of salvaging junk from the home to reuse on the allotment. The guile and flexibility of the small allotment holder therefore are reassuring at a time of mounting unease at supermarket titans and intensive farming methods that seem to dictate what we eat.

Did You Know?

Growing fresh produce on an allotment can save you big money: a trial allotment plot run by the UK Royal Horticultural Society in 1975 produced vegetables and fruit with a value of £240; at today's supermarket prices, that's worth £1,500.

Why Now?

Food prices are going up and carbon footprints must come down. Healthy eating and organic food are zooming up the public agenda. Meanwhile, corner shops are closing and we could be reaching a point where the only place to stock up on food is the out-of-town supermarket.

According to the National Society of Allotment and Leisure Gardeners in the UK, some communities could be at risk of having no access to local food at all in a few years' time. Growing your own fruit and vegetables may become the best if not the only option for many people.

As well as the closing corner shops, pubs are calling last orders for the final time and churches are being sold off to be carved up into luxury flats. Soon, working on the allotment could become the only community activity where people can meet.

Hone Your Expertise

As soon as you get your allotment you will start to enjoy the benefits of growing your own produce and beefing up your knowledge of allotment growing. Opportunities include:

- **Joining an allotment association to help you improve skills and buy materials.**
- **Undertaking allotment gardening courses and weekend workshops.**
- **Talking to fellow plot holders to glean helpful hints and hot tips on growing.**

About This Book

This easy-to-use guide is just the ticket for the budding allotment holder, with all the information you will need to plant, grow, harvest and store vegetables and fruit. It will also tell you how to get started and how to plan and then plant out your plot of land. Sections on preparation, looking after plants, feeding and watering will cover all you need to know to get started and carry on growing on your allotment well into the future.

We can't, sadly, take out all the legwork from tending your plot. But the handy, bite-sized snippets of information within this book should make it a perfect and practical allotment companion for you and your family.

Welcome...

The Green Guide: Allotment Gardening is your essential tool to make working the land as time-saving, trouble free and enjoyable as possible. Growing your own produce is hugely satisfying and the more you grow the more handy hints you'll pick up as you go along.

Dig In

There is no time like the present to get an allotment because the sooner you sow, the faster you will reap a fresh harvest of fruit, vegetables and flowers planted by your own hand. So get out on to that allotment and grab some seed. Plant it, grow it, pick it and eat it.

The Joy of Allotments

Green Shoots of Discovery

More and more people are heading for the allotment and it's not just the whim of a passing trend. People are taking the issue of their food and wellbeing by the bootlaces in the very place you can indulge more than your taste for fresh produce. Allotments are good not only for the food cupboard and the flower vase, but they help your health, pocket and peace of mind too.

Get Physical

With an increased demand for home-grown food and organic lifestyles, many people are turning away from commercially grown crops, and this can invariably lead them to their local allotment site. Allotments are good for people with little or no gardens or large ornamental gardens to get seriously green.

Allotment Aficionado

A plot of land no more than 30 m (98 ft) long can produce a vast array of fruit and vegetables, herbs, cut flowers and other plants for the home. It is the horticultural hub for composting household and garden waste or making friends with other gardeners, and all the time you will be honing your harvesting skills while toning your body to a peak of physical fitness.

In the City

The good thing about allotments is that wherever you go in a town or city you are never far from the telltale patchwork of plots, ramshackle sheds and sundry eccentricities that make allotment life a unique joy. And a good job too. Allotments teach us crucial lessons in sustainability and often form the 'green lungs' or 'green corridors' to the urban canyons of concrete of our cities. They are among the few remaining havens of wildlife and biodiversity to shed light and life on all that drab grey.

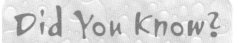

Did You Know?

The average annual cost of an allotment including rent, seeds, compost, fertilizer and pots is a mere £112, according to the UK's National Society of Allotment and Leisure Gardeners.

In the Community

Allotments help nurture connections that go beyond nature too. They do wonders for your social life by acting as communal gathering points for like-minded people to share ideas, catch up on the latest gossip, swap produce and enjoy the occasional night out together.

It is hard to overstate the importance of allotments to our sense of community. In this more introverted age where people rarely have time to talk to their neighbours, allotments form a crucial point of contact. That interaction is as good for mental wellbeing as our communities.

The Extra Dimension

Allotments bring an added dimension to the pleasure of gardening by:

 Ensuring your time is as sociable or as solitary as you want.
Bringing you together with like-minded people bound by a culture of sharing.
Allowing you to tackle a sustainable activity with benefits beyond the allotment.

Preserve and Protect

Allotments offer many ways to attract wildlife that would otherwise struggle to survive on intensively farmed land or in towns and cities. As an individual plot holder you can plant flowers that attract bees and butterflies while the birds lured to your plot will need no invitation to forage for yummy slugs and bugs. Meanwhile, the allotment community is a perfect forum for collective action. This could include digging a shallow pond or gifting an unused plot to wildlife and letting it grow even wilder, with only the occasional trim.

Pests and Guests

Many crop-growing methods protect and respect nature and allow you to do your bit for biodiversity. Lots of larger animals, for example, feed on the aphids and snails you are so keen to banish from your patch. You can encourage 'helpful' wildlife by building bird boxes and hedgehog dens to help keep the more unwelcome guests at bay.

Who's Who

The good guys on your allotment are plentiful and include:

- **Birds:** Bluetits that feed on aphids and caterpillars, thrushes that devour snails and sparrows that feast on weed seeds.
- **Insects:** Spiders that eat flies, earwigs that gobble vine weevil eggs and centipedes that tuck into slugs and their eggs.

Nature Calls

The great thing about allotments and the wildlife they encourage is that you don't have to labour for hours to help nature. And you don't have to worry about the odd patch of long grass or nettles, as these are host plants to a lot of small creatures, such as aphid-gobbling ladybirds. This leaves you more time to cocoon yourself in a productive allotment that teems with wildlife and is all the more enjoyable when you come to relax after a day's harvesting.

Say It With Flowers

Allotments are not the sole domain of fruit and vegetables. Some of the loveliest flowers are the most beneficial to wildlife, so you can enjoy a medley of birds, butterflies and bees along with your beetroot, beans and Brussels sprouts. Feast your senses on these beautiful blooms:

- **Spring**: Choose aubretia, grape hyacinth, primrose and sweet violet.
- **Summer**: Plant buddleia, heather, lavender and verbena.
- **Autumn**: Go for marigold, honeysuckle, sedum and Michaelmas daisy.

Rambling By

Rambling wildlife on the plot is the perfect antidote to the stress and order that governs most of our lives outside the allotment gates. But despite the fears and realities of global warming and pollution, the allotment is one place where creeping urban sprawl is stopped dead in its tracks by your hoe-in-a-row vegetables.

Top Tip

You can make part of your allotment a wildlife habitat by planting low hedging and digging a small pond in the corner, putting up bird boxes and piling up logs to attract hedgehogs and frogs.

Children and Allotments

More young families are discovering the pleasures of spending time on the allotment, which is just how it should be. Children of all ages find allotments dynamic, natural playgrounds; places to root around in the soil and enjoy new sights, sounds and smells. Virtually all children love digging and prodding their fingers in the dirt, so letting them loose on your plot is a terrific way of encouraging them to learn, have fun and exercise.

Plotting an Education

The future of gardening lies with children, and this is especially the case with growing food on allotments. It is widely reported that diets of youngsters are full of junk food and the nearest many come to fresh food is 'vegging' in front of the television.

Giving them a patch of ground will not only keep them busy but teach them where food comes from and how good it tastes fresh from the ground. They will also be given a foretaste of the intriguing world of science, from pollination to perennial plants.

Getting Them Involved

Choose a time when your children are more likely to want to get down on to the allotment such as balmy summer evenings or after homework. Then try to balance growing tasks with fun events like peeling caterpillars from leaves or competitions to identify weeds or bugs. Keep allotment visits short and break them up with a picnic, drinks or lollies.

Allotments for Children

There are many ways to make your plot child friendly. You can:

 Give your children their own small patch of ground to plant and look after.

Kit them out in colourful Wellington boots and give them small tools such as forks and trowels.

Get them to plant easy-to-grow flowers such as nasturtiums and sunflowers.

Mix the flowers in with weird and wonderful vegetables such as pumpkins.

Help them make dens from salvaged wood, corrugated iron, string and bamboo.

Outward Bound

While the outside world may seem threatening to your children, an allotment offers the chance to carve out a haven right on your doorstep, which your youngsters can enjoy with a measure of safety. They can also experience all the good things the larger world has to offer. Sunshine, birds, animals, plants and even a few not-too-boisterous games are all options for the inquisitive, adventurous child. The allotment should suit everyone. It can be an attractive, relaxing place for you as well as a valuable outdoor room that is safe and fun for the kids.

Watch and Work

Allotments and children go well together. Youngsters can grow bored easily yet time rarely stands still on the plot with all that work to do and wildlife to watch. And tinkering with the

recycled throwaway objects that are standard fare on the plot keeps their minds away from eye-wateringly expensive manufactured toys.

Gardening for All

Working together on your allotment is a good way of ensuring that the whole family bonds well together. From sowing the first seeds and enjoying the tasty fruits of your family's labour, allotments offer something for all age groups. And if several families on your site have children, why not ask your landlord to set aside a small area for them to play?

Dos and Don'ts for Children

Your allotment is a peaceful haven not just for you and your family but for others, so:

- **Do**: Make sure your children aren't a nuisance or too noisy; pace of life on an allotment is generally a little slower than in a playground.
- **Do**: Encourage your children to get on their hands and knees and enjoy the whole allotment experience, which involves getting dirty.
- **Do**: Remind youngsters to wash their hands, clear up and brush down tools after they have finished their morning's gardening.
- **Don't**: Let them wander on to other allotments where there may be hazards you or they don't know about.
- **Don't**: Give them lengthy, strenuous tasks such as digging clay soils; break up their day with light, fun tasks.
- **Don't**: Let them damage property on the allotment site or steal the apples and blackberries from Mr Pomfret's allotment!

Top Tip

Great ideas to keep children captivated on an allotment include a 'who can grow the tallest sunflower?' competition or build the wackiest and most effective scarecrow.

Allotments Versus the Big Boys

A number of factors have led to a shift in people's attitude to their food, where it comes from and what's in it. Rising concerns over pesticide residues, intensive farming practices and use of agricultural chemicals have focused the mind on knowing more about what we eat. Allotments are a soothing balm for most of these worries. Produce is local, environmentally friendly and puts you back in control of all aspects of the food-supply chain, from land to larder.

Bad News is Good News

Growing your own fresh produce gives added reassurance in this age of food scares because you know exactly what is going from your plot to the pot. The growing popularity of allotments seems to reflect a declining trust in the corporations that supply most of our food.

Take Your Choice

And even though supermarkets can put fruit and vegetables that are out of season on their shelves, you can be fairly limited on choice. A typical store offers no more than half a dozen types of potato, chosen more for their ability to withstand packing and transport than taste. Allotment growers can choose from hundreds to plant, from King Edward to Pink Fir Apple.

Adding to this unease at who controls our food are the nagging doubts many of us have at the ethics of flying food halfway around the world and clocking up 'food miles'. Eating local produce is better for the environment, while the taste of allotment food is incomparable.

Crunch Time

When the going gets tough, the tough get growing. Vegetable seed sales are outstripping flower seeds for the first time since the English were told to 'Dig for Victory' in the Second World War. Maybe this is driven by uncertainty following the credit crunch. Maybe it is the feeling that in a global economic downturn we need to live more independently. Or maybe it is annoyance at the governments, advertisers and retailers who seem to do everything in their power to coax us to consume more, but rarely encourage us to produce more.

Power to the People

And yet for little more than a few pennies you can buy a packet of seeds that will produce scores of beans, which you can then harvest week after week. It is ironic that the power of the allotment – so vital to our physical and mental survival in the dark days of the Second World War – seems to be re-emerging once more in these times of economic uncertainty.

Age of Reason

Three great social and economic arguments for getting down on to the allotment are:

- It closes the yawning gap between producer and consumer.
- It is great for people tightening their belts and saving money.
- It offers more self-sufficiency and control of chemicals in your food.

Adding Up the Benefits

Allotments can make a big difference to the bottom line as well as your waistline. The standard sized plot should be large enough for a family of four to provide a reasonable amount of their annual needs for fruit and vegetables. This can only be good at a time of rising food costs. Huge amounts of oil are needed to cultivate, fertilize, harvest and transport all our food, yet fuel prices are set to continually rise, pushing up the cost of food even more. Against this background, allotments can be seen as much more revolutionary and socially relevant than the clichéd image of a sleepy provincial pastime suggests.

Food for Thought

In these times of rising prices, increased urbanization and economic pressure, the small green oasis we can create in our allotments is becoming increasingly important. It comes as little surprise to learn that the word 'paradise' comes from the Persian word 'pairidaeza', meaning walled garden.

Fast-food for Thought

Experts have calculated that one 150 g (5 oz) beefburger needs around 2,400 litres (530 gallons) of water to transform the cow grazing in the field to a piece of meat wearing relish in your bun.

Did You Know?

One of the UK's leading conservation groups, the National Trust, recently launched a campaign to create up to 1,000 allotments on its land in England, Wales and Northern Ireland.

skills Base

It is fairly easy to create an allotment garden from which the whole family can enjoy and learn. The skills you pick up are almost endless, from gardening and cultivation tricks to looking after wildlife and dealing with the small potential hazards and risks of the outdoor world.

Allotment Academy

Working on an allotment will help you strengthen your skills across several areas including:

- Teaching yourself how to plant, grow and harvest food.
- Learning about nutrition, food and where it comes from.
- Helping young people learn about nature and food growing.
- Tapping into current issues of sustainability and environmentalism.
- Learning how your body reacts to prolonged exercise and about muscles you never knew even existed before they started to ache the next morning.

Learning Curves

Much of what you learn will be through trial, error and hard graft, but stick the course and you will master hoeing, weeding and planting. You will become a dab hand at pricking out seedlings, testing soil for nutrients as well as learning how to harness the age-old natural cycles of time and the seasons.

Free Time Pays Well

You will also learn how allotments are for people from all walks of life and educational backgrounds. These days we have more free time on our hands than ever before. Allotments make perfect sense for part-time workers, semi-retired people or the unwaged to get outside, brush up their skills and learn a few more.

Endangered Species

Allotments may be growing in popularity but many are under threat. Greedy building developers are for ever eyeing up these tasty morsels of land as potential sites for new houses. Strong demand for allotments from locals like you and me is one of the few ways to let local authorities know how much we love our plots.

Checklist

- ✔ **Allotments have many benefits:** They are good for your health, finances and peace of mind.
- ✔ **A plot of land of around 30 m (98 ft) long is highly productive:** You can grow fruit and vegetables, herbs and spices, cut flowers and other plants for the home.
- ✔ **Allotments teach us important lessons in sustainability:** They are among the few remaining havens of wildlife and biodiversity in our cities.
- ✔ **Working on allotments does wonders for your social life:** You meet like-minded people, share ideas and swap fresh produce.
- ✔ **Everyone can enjoy working on an allotment:** More young families and even children are discovering the pleasures of spending time on the allotment.
- ✔ **You can take more control over your food:** Allotments are good if you worry about pesticide and other chemical residues and intensive farming practices.
- ✔ **You will learn a lot on an allotment:** You can become an expert in hoeing, weeding and planting.

Getting
Started

How and Where

The first thing to do if you are thinking about taking on an allotment is to stop. And then think. It may be tempting to launch into those loamy soils right now but it pays to take your time and to do some research. Allotments can be dotted all over a town or city and waiting lists can be long. But no matter where you live there should be allotments fairly close to hand. Sites are often tucked away behind terraced houses, beside railway lines or on the edges of towns or villages.

Search and You Will Find

Your search will probably start at the heart and bureaucratic soul of the town. Most allotments are owned and run by local authorities, though a few are privately owned. Your first point of contact could be the town hall where they will give you an application form that may ask if you have medical conditions or a disability.

Location, Location, Location

Other good starting points are the local library or town information centre, where you should
be able to find lists of allotment sites and maps to help you pinpoint one close to home.
Location is a crucial factor and you should bear in mind that you may have to carry bulky
and awkward loads to and from your plot or need a space to park your car.

Site Specific

Once you have tracked down the local sites it will pay dividends if you visit the ones
you are interested in. There are many things you need to know about, including:

- **Parking**: This is especially important for elderly people or those with young families.
- **Bicycle sheds**: You don't want a rain-soaked bottom or your bike stolen while
  you work away.
- **Running water**: Most sites have mains water but a few don't, so check there are taps.
- **Loos**: Many sites don't have WCs so some forward planning before each visit
  is a good idea.
- **On-site communal building or shop**: This is a boon should you break a hoe
  or run out of seed.
- **Vandalism**: It's always worth
  checking out the state of boundary
  fences and sheds.

It's Good to Talk

While on your visits, there's nothing like
meeting a plot holder for a chat on what it's
really like on the allotment site. They will also
be able to tell you which plots grow well, where the frost pockets are and which
areas suffer from problems such as wind exposure, flooding or trespassers.

Top Tip

An ideal plot to choose – if choice
is possible – is a south-facing
stretch, which is sheltered from
harsh north winds but has fertile,
free-draining soil and a nearby
source of water.

Go to Ground

Look at the plot, but don't worry too much if allotments have poor earth, as there is nothing a bad soil likes more than a good barrowful of compost or manure. Try to avoid plots overshadowed by buildings or overhanging trees or ones next to weedy sites or overgrown hedges. A well-tenanted site with a happy, lively feel is more likely to be the product of a well-run and well-loved allotment community.

Worth the Wait

The final step is the application, which is fairly likely to prove something of a waiting game. The growing popularity of allotments means some people can be twiddling their thumbs for several months until a plot becomes available, so patience here is a definite virtue. Bear in mind rental periods can run from autumn to autumn, so put your name on the waiting list early.

Don't Lose Heart

That said, in some parts of the country waiting lists have been closed while, in others, local authorities will warn you that you could be waiting for well over a year. But there are still plenty of parts where space is available, especially in more rural areas. Regular calls to your local authority will impress upon the staff at the town hall your eagerness to get stuck in right away.

Moving On Up

Most allotments have associations that hold regular meetings and competitions and organize fund-raising activities. The association chief could be a key ally in your bid to secure an allotment, and if a site manager knows you are raring to go it can be amazing how fast a vacant site suddenly materializes. Offering to help on the site from time to time can also put you in a good light when that dusty waiting list finally sees the light of day.

Keep Plugging Away

There are other things you can do that may improve your chances of securing a coveted allotment plot, such as:

- Agree with the site manager to take on a weedy, overgrown area on the fringe of a site, tame it, make it productive and thereby leapfrog more faint-hearted applicants.
- Apply for plots on several allotment sites within a short distance of each other and see what comes up – you can always turn down a plot if you feel it is unsuitable.
- As a last resort tap up your ward councillor or the local newspaper – land, allotments and gardening strike at the heart of core community values and make terrific news.

Did You Know?

Most local authorities are legally obliged to provide allotment land so if your wait is proving interminable you could always write and ask how it aims to meet its obligation.

Landlord and Tenant

Before walking away with a site key as the proud tenant of a patch of weeds and rickety shed, it's worth finding out what the tenancy agreement involves. The relationship between you and the local authority is that of a landlord and tenant and you both have obligations. The local authority rents the land exclusively to you for a set time and a set rent. You have to look after it!

Read the Small Print

Make sure you keep a copy of the tenancy agreement and, if you are not offered a copy, ask for one. Tenancies are usually granted on an annual basis and are renewable at the end of that period. However, tenancies can be terminated by local authorities on one month's notice if plot holders fall behind on rent.

But forgetful types take heart, the landlord should send out reminder letters before terminating the tenancy, and you should check this with the local authority. If you're in real straits, let the site manager know and alternative payment arrangements may be made. Bear in mind some local authorities offer discounts for retired or unwaged people.

Did You Know?

No tax or business rates are payable on British allotments because in the eyes of the law the plots are seen as agricultural land.

How Allotments Work

Nurturing the fruit and vegetables that will nurture us and our families can be a challenge when it's done on an allotment. As well as the size and location of the plot, other considerations are how much work you will need to dedicate to the plot each week, what the tenancy agreement will demand of you and what you can expect from the landlord.

How Much Do Allotments Cost?

Rental costs for allotments vary enormously, but the one thing they all have in common is they offer superb value for money. Some people pay as little as £5 or £6 a year while others in more well-healed areas can find themselves spending over £100. The average yearly fee hovers somewhere around the £30 mark, and rents are usually collected in one lump at the beginning of the year.

All Part of the Service

Amounts charged often depend on what facilities are on tap such as water, rubbish removal and security. Some local authorities include clearing and rotovating of the plot to help the new plot holder get started and this will be factored into the rental charge. It is always worth asking the landlord or site manager what services are covered in the rental fee and what extras you may have to pay. Remember that local authorities are not legally forced to provide any services at all. And some don't.

Acts of Enclosure

Most allotment plots are between 150 sq m (1,614 sq ft) and 250 sq m (2,700 sq ft), with a typical plot laid out at 25 m (82 ft) long and 10 m (33 ft) wide. This is quite a slice of land for the new plot holder, and many find that taming such a conspicuous brown belt of earth a daunting prospect. Many allotment associations therefore offer half- or even quarter-sized plots. This should ensure that the only furrows go into the ground and not on to the brow of the new face on the allotment. You may also like to consider sharing an allotment – and the workload – with a friend or relative.

Measuring Up

When taking measurements and planning sizes of beds you will need to consider several factors that will affect the overall amount of land you will be able to cultivate:

 Sheds: You may want to build a shed or extend an old one, which will take a sizeable chunk of soil out of production.

 Paths and seating areas: These take land out of action, but are great for defining beds within the plot and, of course, accessing them.

Ponds: If you are allowed a pond by the landlord, they represent another sacrifice of land, but digging them in plot corners can minimize their encroachment.

Laying Down the Law

The plots, sheds and eccentricities that make up your allotment community are defined by rules that can be as quirky as the most curious site characteristic or character. And they can be enforced with varying levels of rigidity. On most sites inspections are carried out by a local authority officer and allotment association leader three or four times a year. The most frequent infringements are messy allotment plots or weed-infested beds, so it's a good idea to spring clean on a regular basis.

Tenancy Terms

Legislation requires some terms to be included in tenancy agreements. These include the length of notice needed to terminate the contract. But the landlord has a fairly free hand to make up its own rules if it thinks they are needed to run the site properly. Many rules vary from site to site.

Some sites allow you to build sheds, ponds and plant fruit trees, others outlaw all of them. Some insist plot holders dedicate nine-tenths of their land to growing only edible produce. The remaining 10 per cent of the plot may be used for growing flowers.

Rule After Rule

Many tenancy agreements include a few basic terms and conditions:

 Plot holders should use the patch as an allotment garden only: Using it as a rave venue, poker den or other business is out, and putting up a slide for children will be frowned upon. Keeping the plot weed free and fit for cultivation instead makes for a quieter life.

Tenants must not annoy or inconvenience a neighbouring plot holder: Blocking or obstructing paths or taps, for example, could land you in hot water with the site manager, and allotment holders should avoid intruding on nearby plots with plants or animals.

Allotment holders cannot construct any building without agreement in writing: Local authorities can throw a strop and force plot holders to take down and remove sheds put up without the prior nod from council officials, which may have rules on size and materials used.

Existing boundary hedges, ditches and fences next to your plot must be looked after: This can be messy work and involve clearing ditches of silt and supermarket trolleys or whipping out a hammer and nails to patch up a rickety wooden fence.

Livestock is banned apart from animals allowed by law, such as rabbits and hens: However, pigs, goats and even bees have found their way on to allotments. But unless the local authority has given its approval and inspected hutch or hive, expect another angry letter.

Top Tip

It's a good idea to look at the rule book before signing a tenancy agreement to make sure there are no sticking points or clauses that could really bug you.

Manners, Please

As well as the hard-and-fast rules of an allotment site, don't forget the allotment community is a tight-knit and friendly collective. Allotment etiquette is almost as important a code of conduct as the written rules. You wouldn't dream of snaffling Bert's prize marrows, but you should also be considerate of other things.

Top Tip

It is useful to remember that the allotment plot is on communal land; behaviour therefore ought to be tempered and not tempestuous.

Peas and Qs – Mind Them

It always helps to consider fellow allotment users' needs and wants. Use chemicals such as weedkiller subtly and sensitively if you know your neighbour is nurturing an organic plot, and think twice about lighting a bonfire on a busy or windy day. If, on the other hand, you really want to annoy your crotchety neighbour, try hogging the communal water supply for 45 minutes. Job done.

More Manners from Heaven

Keep your plot neat and tidy and avoid leaving piles of rubbish or weeds on paths. You could also do yourself a favour by:

- Taking an active part in allotment life and sharing your seeds, food and flowers.
- Avoiding planting hedges or other tall plants that may shade next door's plot.
- Always asking before switching on the radio or jacking up the volume on your hi-fi.

What to Look Out For

Choosing a plot with good facilities close to hand and easy access can make the difference between success or demoralizing failure, so it pays to be a little choosy. And it may be worth holding back and counting to 10 when the first offer of an allotment rolls in. Is it close enough to home, for example? You are far more likely to make a decent fist of your plot if it's within a fairly short walking distance, bike ride or drive from your house or flat.

Seize the Moment

Before you take on an allotment you should also ponder one of the most important considerations: how much time should I spend, and how much time can I spend, on the plot?

The more hours you eke out on the land, the more you will achieve and the more productive both you and your plot will be. Ideally you should spend half an hour each day digging and hoeing, but if this is out of the question, you really need to visit the site at least once a week to keep on top of the weeds, if nothing else.

Top Tip

Think about holidays, bank holidays and Christmas: if you take a break you will probably have to ask a neighbouring plot holder to keep an occasional eye on your beans and asparagus and water them when needed.

In the Shade

A little shade on your plot is a good thing, especially in the summer months when the heat is beating down on everything, including you. But it is better to have a measure of control by putting up some form of shelter rather than have shelter imposed upon you in the form of a large tree or building. You should check how much sun your plot will catch throughout the day. Large trees not only hog the light, their roots can soak up all the nutrients in the soil, leaving your plants nothing but a few scraps.

Straight and Narrow

You should also look out for the flattest plot on the site. A sloping site will feel even steeper when you are struggling with a barrow full of manure or compost. Not only are sloping sites hard to get around, but they tend to have drainage problems – arid on top, boggy at the bottom. You are also more likely to find something else lurking at the bottom of a sloping site – frost. Allotments that trail off into low ground can suffer from the big chill, as cold edges its way into valleys and depressions. Try to remember:

- ☑ If the plot slopes to the north, the soil will be colder and take longer to warm.
- ☑ If it slopes to the south, it is likely to retain warmth well into autumn.

Top Tip

Don't feel obliged to take the first plot you are offered by the site manager, who may be trying to fob you off with the worst, and never say yes to a plot without looking at it first.

Top of the Plots

Regardless of whether your plot is on a slight slope or overshadowed in one corner by a tree, it is good to look at your plot as an evolving masterpiece. If you take on a full plot, you can put a third or even a half on hold while you get stuck into the remainder. This will make your workload more manageable, but you'll have to keep an eye on the weeds from time to time.

Take the Strain

Managing your workloads is as important as choosing the right site. Gardening is great exercise, but think about your own levels of fitness before taking on a large plot. Some soils can be murderously hard to work, but taken at your own pace you'll soon build up strength.

Safe and Secure

One of your first jobs when starting out should be a quick visual once over of the site to check for potential hazards. But try to look at minor risk as something not altogether bad. Allotments can be places where children can learn to look after themselves and each other, for example.

Make Checks

It is also a good idea to check the vaccination status of everyone in your family to protect from tetanus, a bacterial disease that can be caught when a grazed knee or cut finger touches soil. The golden rule with children on allotments is to keep them occupied, but keep an occasional eye on them.

Keep Them Out

Don't forget your allotment hardware can be a soft target for thieves, so one of your first tasks could be to check there is not only somewhere to store your tools, but that they won't vanish overnight. If you have a shed, fit sturdy locks. If you rely on a communal store to park your spades after a hard day's graft, a whip-round among allotment holders will pay for locks.

Wired Up

Using barbed wire could land you in trouble with the landlord. Some allotments ban barbed or razor wire, especially if it is strung up next to a path used by other plot holders. This is to prevent others from snagging their clothing or themselves on the wire and could make you liable for their injury.

- **Get into the habit of knowing where your tools are at all times and avoid leaving them lying around on the plot when not being used.**
- **Mark your tools in a bold way; this will not only make them easier to pick out in an identity parade of spades, but make them less attractive to thieves.**
- **Think about fitting a battery-operated alarm to your shed, but make sure it works properly and don't annoy residents or plot holders with nuisance alarms or frequent sound checks.**
- **Ask other allotment holders what problems they have had with vandals and thieves and what security measure they have resorted to.**

Be Positive

Allotments can be like gold dust and waiting lists long, but people often fall out of the pecking order because they move or lose interest. You may be pleasantly surprised. Likewise, messy plots are no match for a little dedication from their new taskmaster.

Checklist

✔ **Where to start**: Your search for an allotment may start at the town hall, library or town information centre.

✔ **It pays to visit sites and talk to plot holders**: Getting on to the site will give you a clearer idea of what you are letting yourself in for.

✔ **Don't lose heart**: Keep phoning up the local authority to impress upon them how keen you are for an allotment now.

✔ **Cost**: The average yearly fee for an allotment is around the £30 mark, and rents are usually collected in one lump at the beginning of the year.

✔ **Size**: Most allotment plots are between 150 sq m (1,614 sq ft) and 250 sq m (2,700 sq ft), with a typical plot laid out at 25 m (82 ft) long and 10 m (33 ft) wide.

✔ **Rules and etiquette**: Allotments are governed by a series of rules, and their close-knit communities rely on a strong code of etiquette.

✔ **How much time will my plot take up?** Ask yourself how much time can I spend and should I spend on the plot?

✔ **Plot characteristics to look out for**: Is your allotment overshadowed by buildings or trees and is it flat or on a slope?

Planning Your Plot

Soil

Soil is the foundation on which your success, or otherwise, on the allotment depends. So get to know it. A good understanding of the earth beneath your feet will make your life on top of it much easier. If you're lucky, it will be fertile. This is more likely if the plot has been lying unused for some time allowing the soil to revitalize itself from past cultivation. If, however, you have inherited a well-worked plot, the soil may be all but exhausted and need a helping hand from you.

On Your Knees

The quickest, easiest and perhaps most enjoyable way of striking up an acquaintance with your soil is to sink to your knees. Grab a handful of Mother Earth and touch it, feel it, look at it. This will give you some idea of its qualities, which will help you appreciate its needs.

Which is Which?

All soil is made up of organic matter, which means dead animals and plants, and three main mineral elements. You should be able to identify them by rubbing the soil in your hands to give an indication of what type of soil you have. If it feels:

 Loose and light and sifts easily through your fingers: You have a sandy soil.

 Heavy and moist and easily balls in your fingers: You have a clay soil.

 Silky, looks slightly shiny and retains moisture more than sand: You have a silty soil.

Mix and Match

Most soils are a mixture of the three main types, but it is important to know which element is richest in your soil. This will affect the kind of crops you can grow and what level of success you can expect. The good news is that you can make changes to the soil to make it easier to work and therefore more productive. This is very important because allotment soil can be next to useless and quagmire in winter only to develop a hard, impervious crust in the heat of summer.

Sand

It's a good idea to get to know the qualities of your particular soil type. Sandy soil is much easier to dig than clay, and water – like the sand through your fingers – disperses more freely after a downpour. Though it will not waterlog in winter, it tends to dry out in summer and, because of its loose, easily draining structure, nutrients wash away along with the rain.

Clay

Clay soils are heavy, cloying and stick to your spade, making them harder to work than other soils. They are damp and shiny and slow to warm up, which can delay sowing times. They tend to get waterlogged in winter and form a tough crust in summer. Now the good points: clay holds water and nutrients really well, making it a rich and fertile soil.

Silt

The fine grains that characterize silty soil make it a free-draining alternative to clay. It is easy to dig and has a higher level of nutrients than sandy soils but lower than clay. However, it is easily tramped to a hard, compacted surface after a good drenching, so it tends to need lots of working and a helping hand in the form of organic matter such as manure.

More Soil Types

As well as the three main soil types – clay, sand and silt – there are other kinds, which include the best. Loamy soil is as near to perfect a balance of clay, sand and silt as you can probably get. It is easy to dig and drain, crumbly to touch and high in nutrients. Sadly, it is hard to find. Other soils include:

Chalky: They have white clumps of chalk or flint and tend to dry out in summer.

 Peaty: These are common to the Fens and East Anglia, and are rich, fertile and wet.

DIY Soil Test

Half fill an empty jam jar with water and top it up with soil. Screw on the lid, give it a good shake and leave for a couple of days: sand – the heaviest constituent – will sit on the bottom below silt, with clay on top. This will give you an instant idea of the make-up of your soil.

Sit and Watch

You can also tell a great deal about your soil in the comfort of your allotment shed with the rain lashing down outside. If the rainwater pools on the surface of the plot it is a telltale sign you have clay. If, on the other hand, the water drains away quickly you are likely to have a sandy soil. Sometimes you may find your allotment has patches of different soil types.

Organic Gardening

Understanding the different soil types can be quite confusing, but fortunately each one of them can be improved in much the same way – with liberal amounts of organic matter, such as well-rotted farmyard manure or garden compost dug into your allotment plot.

Dirt Digging

Your number one aim is to achieve a consistency of soil that resembles that rich and crumbly loam you were so hoping to find on your plot. Manure or compost will help lighter soils retain water and nutrients, while adding it to heavier soils will open them up to ease drainage.

Soil Without the Spoil

Digging organic matter into clay will help break up its tight structure, allowing water and air to circulate more freely. Meanwhile, adding organic material to your sandy soil will help bulk it out to retain moisture and nutrients.

Down on the Farm

Organic material comes in many forms; just look at all those large, colourful 70 litre bags stacked up in the corner of your garden centre filled with green, spent-mushroom and leaf composts. But you can also check out your business phone directory for nearby stables and livery yards. Some will give you horse manure; others will even deliver it for free. But remember the golden rule: use only well-rotted manure, as the ammonia in fresh dung can harm plants.

Good Chemistry

Having found out the type of your earth, you still have some soil sleuthing to do to find out whether it is an acidic or alkaline soil. This will also affect how the fruit, vegetables and flowers on your allotment grow, and the measurement is made on a scale of 0 to 14 called the pH scale. Acid soils are below pH 7, alkaline above.

Optimum Digging Time

Heavy or clay soils are best dug in the autumn in readiness for the winter onslaught of rainfall, to enable the soil to drain more freely.

On the Scales

But tip the scales too far either side and your soil could have problems. Brassicas, for example, do not like too much acid while rhubarb is more tolerant. A very high or low pH level can prevent plants from absorbing nutrients, even in nutrient-rich soils. You can remedy too acidic a soil by digging in lime. Alkaline-rich soils are harder to treat but growing and harvesting may slowly bring the alkalinity down.

Eye Level

If this all sounds too scientific, go to your garden centre and pick up an inexpensive soil-testing kit. It's easy to test your soil and it will give you important information to help you plan which crops you want to grow. The kit includes:

 A solution: This is added to a sample of soil in a test tube.

A colour chart: This is used to match the colour of the solution to a pH chart.

What and When

Clay soils, characterized by richness in nutrients, are happy to settle for low-nutrient compost, but for lighter, poorer soils you should go for richer compost to give it a helping hand when you come to plant your fruit, vegetables and flowers. Most crops also enjoy a good raking in of compost about once a year.

Did You Know?

Most vegetables do well in a neutral soil, the optimum being around pH 6.5.

Digging in manure can be a strenuous task, but try not to put off the job. A little soil enrichment can help the productivity of your soil and turn it from a heavy, cloggy mess into a crumbly, nutrient-packed bed from which you can harvest prize-winning produce year after year.

Remember

There is a big difference between feeding the soil and feeding your beloved plants, but both are important if you are to achieve the best results. Though soil is hardly the most thrilling aspect of your allotment, that earth beneath your feet is absolutely essential to good crops and is one of the few things in your allotment you can directly influence.

In Your Dreams

Rare indeed is the allotment holder who reckons their soil is perfect. But in an ideal world, the ideal allotment soil would be rich in nutrients and organic matter, well-drained but retaining plenty of moisture. It would be well aerated with plenty of worms and biological activity, slightly acid or neutral and with a good crumbly soil structure.

Never Miss a Chance

You should never miss an opportunity to improve your allotment soil because a happy plant is a well-fed and healthy plant. The organic material you use on your patch will also delight earthworms, as they drag nutrients down into the soil, eat them and produce even more nutritious matter.

You won't be able to grow worthwhile vegetables, fruit and flowers in your allotment unless the soil is fertile, so it really does pay to get to know it, and be patient: even the best soil needs close attention and careful nurturing – just like those plants of yours.

How to Decide What to Grow

Fruit and vegetables are essential to life while flowers bring colour and happiness to our living rooms. Fortunately, the range of plants we can grow is enormous and whether you are a beginner or skilled allotment gardener, you will find raising plants from tiny seeds to full-blown maturity both culturally and nutritionally rewarding. The fun of allotment growing lies in the freshness of plants and seeing the small investment in plot rental and seeds pay handsomely on the table.

Starting Fresh

Once you have cleared your plot you will probably see what appears to be a vast barren plateau of brown stretching into infinity. The feeling of all that space is likely to be especially acute if you live in a town or city with nothing more than a tiny backyard or garden the size of a postage stamp. You couldn't be more wrong.

Plants take up space almost as fast as you can eat them. So it's a good idea to draw up a list of what you like and your nutritional needs. An interesting balance between succulent fruits, bulky vegetables and bright splashes of colour from flowers rarely goes amiss.

Time Out

Now is the time to settle down with a mug of tea or coffee, or something stronger, and a pile of seed catalogues. Why not get each person in the family to choose two or three favourite plants, which will ensure their vested interest in the allotment?

It's a Seasonal Thing

It's a good idea before you start buying and scattering your seeds randomly to draw up a rough plan of your plot and where you want the vegetables to go. Forward planning in such a visual way will help you divide the space. It will also give you an idea of what you have to play with to squeeze in your Swiss chard, shallots and potatoes and leave enough space for some bee-attracting sweet peas.

Good Value Plants

The best value fruit and vegetables are the ones you love to eat most, while the finest flowers are the ones you simply can't do without arranged in a vase on a summer's day. But there are other factors to consider. Ease of planting and caring is a major plus point. And fruit and vegetables that taste their crispest from the soil always beat their limp, prepacked supermarket alternatives hands down.

Not So Good Value Plants

Plants don't always represent great value on the allotment in time and money.
A vegetable may take up a lot of space, take a long time to grow or produce sluggish
yields. It may also fall prey more easily than others to pests and diseases. Or maybe that
celery in the greengrocer is just so cheap you feel it makes more sense to dig into your
pocket than your soil.

Time, Please

A really important consideration on what plants to grow on your plot is time. If you are
pushed for it, why not think about growing lower-maintenance crops like allotment stalwarts
such as potatoes and broad beans. Cross off your list plants that demand harvesting every
few days, such as some of the salad crops.

Easy Tiger

Allotment virgins take note – don't be too adventurous. Few things are more disheartening
to even the most ardent allotment holders than losing control of your crops. Start with a
limited plant palette and soften yourself up with a few easy-to-grow vegetable choices.
Spinach, lettuce, sweetcorn and leeks will do
nicely and you could throw in a few
interesting choices like pumpkin.

Eating Into Time

Vegetables such as these require little effort
but produce bumper crops. Plants like
tomatoes, on the other hand, can be tricky,
requiring a frame to support them, shelter and
constant pinching out. Take into account how much time – realistically – you can spend on the
plot on a regular basis, especially if you have children. Your allotment is supposed to be a
pleasure to behold, not a cross to bear.

Top Tip

**Keeping a close eye on what
and where you grow on your plot
and referring to your hand-drawn
plan should help solve the
problem of lost labels.**

A Healthy Choice

Another factor to think about when you are choosing what to stock on your plot is nutrition and the health needs of you and your family. Diets rich in fruit and vegetables are associated with lower illness risks. Bearing in mind it is recommended we eat at least five portions a day, this could give you a good yardstick of what to grow and how much to plant in your allotment. Remember:

- Fruit and vegetables are rich in carbohydrates, dietary fibre, vitamin C, folic acid and potassium.
- Diets packed with fruit and vegetables will help people in your family who have health problems like high blood pressure, tiredness or cardiovascular trouble.
- Broccoli and sweet potatoes are rich in vitamin A and good for people with poor night vision or dry skin.
- Green leafy vegetables and asparagus are bulked out with folic acid, which is good at combating anaemia and loss of appetite.
- Potatoes and other leafy vegetables are big on vitamin B, which can help people with lack of energy or depression.

Vegetables Equal Vitamins

Vegetables contain most of the vitamins we need, but as soon as they are picked their vitamin content dwindles, so eat them soon after picking. Don't worry if you have a glut, freezing vegetables will lock in some of those vitamins.

Keep Rowing

If you eat only a couple of courgettes a month, it is fairly pointless planting out two 3 m (10 ft) rows of them. Focusing your mind on what your needs are is a good way of avoiding a glut of tomatoes or beetroot at the end of the season. Some people team up with other plot holders to share out who grows what, but growing one particular plant can be dull.

Take It Easier

While there is no such thing as a low-maintenance allotment, you can make life much easier if you:

 Choose crops that are both low-maintenance and offer good ground cover.

Cover your soil when it's not in use to keep the weeds from poking through.

Mulch the earth on a regular basis to help the soil lock in its moisture.

Cover paths in polythene or old carpet and salvaged pavers to keep out the weeds.

Make raised beds and fill them with compost to save you having to dig too much.

Make a Note

Keeping an allotment diary and noting what you grow each season will prove a real boon. That way you will remember when you last planted leeks, what a poor crop of courgettes you had two years ago and how wonderful those beetroot were last year.

Layout

When it comes to designing your allotment you have a careful balancing act on your hands. Your plot must be functional and smooth running. It must enable you to saunter freely between beds and make a beeline for the shed without traipsing over the seedbed or dunking your foot in the pond. Just putting a compost bin in the nearest corner and hurling a few seeds on the ground won't do. You need to plan ahead and think visually as well as in terms of metres and feet.

Different Aspects

A big priority point is access. This is in terms of entering the allotment site, reaching your plot and then moving around the patch. Don't forget there will be days when you are heavily laden with tools, and you will need logical and cohesive access paths to ensure you don't stumble over the communal tap.

More Aspects

Other important considerations are:

- ☑ **Aspect:** Which way does the plot face?
- ☑ **Existing features:** Are there nearby trees, buildings, pathways and taps?
- ☑ **Wind:** Where does the prevailing wind come from?

Scaling Up

If weighing up all the priorities is proving a little daunting, it's a great idea to draw a small-scale plan of your site on a piece of graph paper. Measurements don't have to be down to the nearest centimetre or inch, but they should be to the nearest square metre or square foot.

Marking Out

Measure the boundaries of your site and transfer them to the graph paper, sketching in all the existing features, such as trees. There may be bits and bobs on the plot you want to keep, such as an old shed or fruit cage, in which case draw them on to the sheet as well. This will give you an outline plan, the blank spaces of which you can now fill in with your beds and other features.

When this plan is finished you should have a sheet of paper with a series of boxes marked on it to show the different beds, seating area, compost zone and paths. Transferring the rectangular doodles of this outline plan into reality will involve a tape measure, stakes and string or grass spray, which you can buy from garden or DIY centres.

Mucking In

If you're new to allotment gardening, it is perhaps a good idea to stick to a basic layout, which is simple to build. For now it may be prudent to leave the circular herb-edged beds to more experienced hands. An easier plot to handle usually has a symmetrical layout of eight to 12 beds divided by a path running down the middle of the plot. The shed is tucked away in a corner and the compost area falls nicely into place in a shady central nook for easy access.

Jockeying for Position

What plants you choose will depend on your taste. If you like fruit, then a quarter or thereabouts of your plot could be dedicated to edible berries and fruit trees, if the landlord allows the latter. This permanent planting should be complemented with beds for annual vegetables and a cut-flower garden for those blooms. Favourite vegetables, which you are likely to want to eat most days in season, will, of course, need more space to grow on your allotment.

Take Your Places

You should also consider where on your allotment you want to plant your star performers. Fragrant flowers such as the climbers scrambling over your shed and the rosemary in the herb patch next to your seating area will make for a more sensually evocative place to rest your weary bones.

Mixing In

Plants on an allotment can jostle fairly comfortably together, though it pays to keep the permanent beds together.

Top Tip

Whatever you grow, if you can run the beds from north to south you will give your crops even levels of sunlight.

Fruit bushes are paradise for birds so it makes a lot of sense to keep them under one fruit cage. There are many schools of thought on how allotments should be laid out, but as long as it is workable – be in it raised wooden beds, rows or blocks – it shouldn't really matter.

Rush Hours

You are now ready to think about the seasons and what they mean for you as an allotment workhorse. Things start happening from March to July, so expect to spend an hour or so nearly every day on the plot. You will find yourself digging, preparing beds and sowing seeds. You will also be attacking weeds as well as mending all the winter-weather damaged parts of the allotment, such as repainting the shed and repairing the wooden compost enclosure.

In Summertime

From August onwards – if you're lucky – the backbreaking work is behind you and all you need to do is water your fruit, vegetables and flowers. Don't forget to make friends with fellow plot holders and ask them to water your plants if you take a weekend break. Late autumn will see you clearing up the beds, tidying the allotment and more digging.

In the Bleak Midwinter

In darkest winter you may be able to ratchet down numbers of visits to the allotment, but there are chores to be going on with, such as digging – if conditions allow – and uprooting a few cabbages, leeks or onions. This is also a great time to rake in manure or compost. You may get away with a couple of visits a month from December to late February.

Planning a Crop Rotation

Ever get bored of the same place? So do crops, which is where crop rotation enters the fray. Plants grown in exactly the same plot will yield poorer harvests as the years go by because soil-borne pests and diseases build up. And like people, different crops thrive off or need different nutritional balances. Plant brassicas in the same plot, for example, and nitrogen levels in the soil will dwindle, leaving the plants a sickly pallor in following years.

Turning Full Circle

Throw the planting regime in the air, however, and something else happens – the plants can thrive. Crop rotation is the practice of growing vegetables in different parts of the allotment from year to year. This preserves the balance between the nutrients in the soil and makes plants less likely to fall ill.

You do not have to follow a rigid system, but it's a good idea to bear in mind what went into the ground last year and banish that crop to another part of the allotment this year. That said, well-organized plot holders often find an ordered and systematic crop rotation that runs like clockwork immeasurably rewarding.

Watching the Years Go By

Crop rotation is often planned out on three- to five-year cycles, depending on how many vegetables you want to plant and how much space you have.

First Stage

The first step is to make a list of all the vegetables you want to grow on your allotment and then put them into their various categories. The three main categories are legumes, such as beans; brassicas, including cabbage and cauliflower; and root vegetables such as carrots, swedes and turnips. Each group has different wants and needs from the soil.

Here is an example of the seamless jigsaw that nature can be. Legumes are known as nitrogen 'fixers'. They draw nitrogen from the air and disperse it into the soil through their roots. Brassicas need lots of nitrogen from the soil to thrive, so it makes sense to plant them a year after legumes have been in the bed.

Second Stage

Divide your plot into sections and plant them out. Your first bed could be home for the next year for your root vegetables, so dig in your parsnips, potatoes and carrots. Next come the legumes of your choice, perhaps broad beans, peas and endives. That leaves the third bed and the brassicas: cabbages, cauliflowers and kohlrabi.

Don't Forget

Remember to leave aside enough land for your permanent crops like fruit bushes, flowers and specialist plants such as aubergines and peppers.

What to Grow

One of the best things about taking on an allotment is choosing what you grow. In your earlier years this may be more about trial and error than personal preference. A good maxim is to avoid overplanting. By harvesting little and often you will avoid a vegetable glut and the resulting waste of produce. Keeping it small and simple will also ensure you enjoy everything in peak condition, when it's bursting with flavour and goodness.

Think about what you and your family enjoy eating and plant a few seeds, ensuring you have vegetables for each season. Check the seed packets; some vegetables are marked 'early', 'maincrop' and 'late', and this should enable you to choose crops over a long period of time. Onions are usually planted in early to mid spring; wild rocket and some types of lettuce often grow a treat when sown around September.

Variety is the Spice of Life

The variety of the plant or cultivar can make all the difference. Each plant on your allotment may exist in different forms, chosen by breeders over the years and boasting specific characteristics. Some vegetable varieties, for example, have been bred with resistance to blight, including tomato 'Ferline'.

Top Tip

Seeds need the best possible growing conditions: warm temperature, good light levels, moisture and good ventilation.

Name Calling

Some of the most interesting varieties are from the heritage or heirloom vegetables. They are the age-old favourites sold by specialist suppliers that boast fantastic names like 'Drunken Woman' lettuce. These beauties are a bit of a mixed bag, are pollinated by natural means, such as wind, insects or birds, and offer more variable shapes and colours. But they can be more prone to diseases.

'First Filial'

In the opposite corner to the heritage varieties are the so-called F1 hybrids. These commercially produced seeds differ from the heritage varieties in that they are artificial crosses between two genetically different varieties. This results in unwanted genetic characteristics being bred out to ensure a purer strain. Though offering vigour, F1 seeds are expensive and can be used only once. This is because the second generation of the plants will not come true.

Sourcing Seeds

Where F1 hybrids have become standard fare in seed catalogues, strict rules govern the availability of heritage varieties. The Heritage Seed Library, which is part of the British organic charity Garden Organic, has been nurturing hundreds of varieties since the 1970s. Members, needless to say, are avid seed swappers. It is also a good idea to check out the internet, small independent nurseries or the back of gardening magazines for suppliers of more unusual ranges.

Closer to Home

A ready source of seeds may be closer to home. Several allotment sites run seed exchanges from their communal building. Growers with a bounty of seed from a favourite crop sign up, list what they've got and then check out what you've got. If they like what they see, a swap is on the cards.

Ask Around

No matter how experienced an allotment gardener you are, sowing seed is tricky. Not all vegetable varieties may be suitable for your soil conditions. This is where the advice of seasoned growers on your allotment site could prove invaluable, for they will probably have a good idea which varieties grow best in that area. If you doubt their wisdom, check out their whopping leeks and marrows at the next parish fête. They invariably know what they are talking about.

Not Going to Seed

Most allotment growers raise their plants from seed, but garden centres now offer vegetable plants such as tomatoes and aubergines. If allotment time is tight or you only want one or two of these kinds of plants, this may be a better route.

Permanent Features

Permanent structures such as sheds, greenhouses and compost bins often form both the visual and productive heart of the allotment. In a shed you can store tools, seeds and even yourself when all you want is a little peace and quiet. Most permanent structures such as greenhouses come in easy-to-build flat packs, but the iconic image of the allotment shed is the do-it-yourself variety, thrown together from offcuts of wood, old guttering and tarpaulin.

Sheds

Sheds are more than homes for your tools; they play an important part in the functioning of your plot. Their walls can offer shelter to more tender plants while the guttering that feeds into water butts can be used for irrigation. Cabins of 12 sq m (130 sq ft) should be big enough for most allotment holders' needs, according to the UK National Society of Allotment and Leisure Gardeners. If you can't lay a thin concrete slab, it is a good idea to build the shed on bricks to keep it off the earth and allow air to circulate underneath.

Top Tip

Don't forget to check with your landlord what permanent structures – if any – you are allowed, and also ask if there are restrictions on size, materials and type of foundations, such as concrete slabs.

Climbers

Your shed will take up quite a large part of your plot so it seems a shame not to make it pay for its keep. All that vertical space in the form of wooden walls is perfect for climbing plants. All you need to do is to screw in a few hooks and string up some garden wire, then watch those rampant ramblers take hold. Some good climbing plants include:

- **Hops:** Hops are beautiful to look at and, even if you are not into brewing your own beer, you can cook the leaves or eat them raw.
- **Honeysuckle:** This will twine and lash itself up your home-made trellis and is a true climber with a fragrance to set your nose twitching in anticipation.
- **Roses:** Climbing roses thrust their strong stems up your wire framework, but will need to be kept in check with pruning.

Greenhouses

In the greenhouse you can overwinter tender plants that will spend the summer months outside. You can bring on plants for the house and conservatory and you can raise seedlings and root cuttings, grow tomatoes, melons, cucumbers and aubergines, even a stone fruit or two. It's good to avoid building greenhouses at the foot of slopes as low ground often acts as a frost pocket.

Atmosphere is Everything

Hitting on the right atmospheric conditions is your number one goal with a greenhouse. For your tomatoes and flower seeds to flourish you want air that is humid but not stagnant, which is why you should make sure your structure has ridge vents as well as opening windows. From late spring to the end of a good summer you will probably have to open them to ensure a good flow of air around the plants. You should also consider buying blinds, because when the sun gets too hot it may scorch your plants.

Walk-on Parts

An earth floor under your slatted greenhouse benches can be colonized by shade-loving plants, which soak up water spillage from irrigation in summer; if the whole floor area is paved it will be harder to keep up humidity in the warmer months.

Paths

A good path will not only offer easier access to your produce, but will help show off those well-kept beds to their best. Old timber slats, concrete pavers or bark chippings from a local tree surgeon all make good surfacing for paths, but remember to make them wide enough for wheelbarrows.

If you aim to build or improve a path, make sure you lay the paving on a well-drained base of firm, level and compact soil. A layer of polythene or old carpeting laid underneath a heavy surface such as concrete paving should keep the weeds out.

Windbreaks

We've all seen them from our train windows or on our canal-side walks – exposed and wind-buffeted allotments taking everything Mother Nature can throw at them. While we allotment holders can go into the shed and reach for the Thermos flask and biscuits, our plants are not so lucky. Cold wind can scorch leaves and snap stems.

Shelter

Fortunately there are several things we can do. Semi-solid barriers such as woven willow or even wooden pallets turned on their sides make good windbreaks. The idea is to slow down the wind rather than check it suddenly causing vortexes and turbulence. Hedging or long grass can make excellent windbreaks, which ought to be fast growing yet sturdy, well anchored to the soil and able to survive exposure. Other natural windbreaks are:

- Blackberry bushes.
- Raspberry bushes.
- Gooseberry bushes.
- Fruit trees such as pear.

Putting Up Barriers

You may need permission from your landlord to put up a barrier, but forget about building a wall. This is one of the least effective windbreaks, as gales smack into the wall, gust over the bricks and barrel down the other side to cause chaos to your plants.

Top Tip

Cold wind is one of the biggest killers of early crops, so think about windbreaks sooner rather than later.

Compost Bins

The compost heap is the engine room of your allotment, supplying the essence of life to your soil in the form of organic matter. It also strikes at the heart of the recycling ethos held so dear by plot holders. Not only does it find a use for all your garden waste – grass cuttings, hedge clippings, old plants – but you can make

the compost bin itself from recycled materials, such as old pallets strung or nailed together to form an open-fronted slatted box with a pallet for a base.

Make Do

As well as slats, you can make compost bins out of breeze blocks, bricks, wood panels and straw bales. These materials all offer good insulation and by putting broken bricks or brushwood at the bottom you will ensure drainage and aeration and encourage worms to move into the compost.

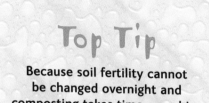

Top Tip

Because soil fertility cannot be changed overnight and composting takes time, your bins must be sturdy enough to withstand the long haul of decomposition, which can take from six months to a year.

You can also buy purpose-made plastic bins from garden centres, but this goes against the grain for some allotment holders, who wear their recycling credentials like a badge of honour. If all this is too much trouble, you can settle for a rough-and-ready pile of vegetable and flower waste and cover it with a plastic sheet until the plant material has decomposed.

Fences

By their nature, allotments are open so even if your landlord allows you to build a solid fence around all or part of your allotment, it may not go down well with your plot neighbours. A good and cheaper alternative is fencing made of chicken wire. Put it up and in no time at all brambles and grass are clinging to the metal, slowing down the wind and offering a welcome home to insects and other wildlife.

Hedges

Hedges have three big advantages: they make great boundaries, they are super windbreaks and they look so much better than fencing or other man-made barriers. The only drawback is they have to be looked after to stop them straggling on to neighbouring plots. You should check with your landlord that planting hedging is allowed and then:

- **Plant evergreen hedging in spring or autumn and deciduous in autumn or winter.**
- **One of the simplest ways of planting is to dig the hedging into a 30 cm (1 ft) wide trench of equal depth.**
- **If your allotment is very exposed you may have to drive in posts every 2–3 m (6½–10 ft).**

Planning Ahead

Like all things on the allotment, plan ahead. With all forms of boundary, find out which way the prevailing wind blows: coldest and strongest generally come from the northeast.

Small Details

As well as the mainstays like sheds and greenhouses, your allotment will also benefit from some smaller items:

Water butt: These are crucial if you don't have a nearby water source, and can be bought from garden centres as plastic or wooden barrels. The quickest, easiest and most effective way of filling them is by running a drainpipe from your shed eaves into the butt. Plants love rainwater and it's a lot less hassle than trailing a hose or fetching water from a communal tap 50 m (160 ft) away.

 Coldframes: These compact glass-roofed boxes enable allotment growers to bring plants on early and harden them off. Ideally the roof should slope 30 degrees to maximize the amount of daylight reaching the plants, and they are easy to make from bricks or slats of wood with an old salvaged window on top.

 Leaf-mould bin: You can make a leaf-mould bin by driving four stakes into the ground and securing chicken wire around the uprights. Fill it up with fallen leaves in autumn and leave them to compost for a year – the resulting mixture makes a terrific compost or soil improver.

 Old bath or pond: Anything that collects and stores water is a godsend to an allotment grower. Water also attracts beneficial wildlife, and the creatures encouraged by a pond will help with pest control in the growing season. Remember to put the plug in the bath!

 Seat: A wooden bench, folding metal seat or plastic chair will form the perfect vantage point to relax and admire all your hard work.

Edging Boards

Edging boards are a good way of dividing paths from the beds on your allotment and can make the plot look and function much better. Use old floorboards, logs, scaffold planks or railway sleepers to keep soil off the paths and loose path materials off the soil. They also allow you to improve soil in localized areas. And if your beds are narrow enough, you won't have to tread on them to reach across and therefore damage plants or compact the soil.

Care and Repair

Your sheds and greenhouses will be as good as the care and upkeep you lavish on them. Find a corner inside to store some paint for the odd touching-up job, some wood preserver for that old fence and window putty in case of a breakage.

Chopping and Changing

Try to avoid micro-managing your allotment. Your plot is never 'finished', and one of the most enjoyable things about creating and looking after that patch is that you can enjoy a fair amount of flexibility with your planting and features. Unless you want to grow in raised beds, which are made of wooden planks boxed to hold compost, most vegetables can be moved every year.

Checklist

- **Get to know your soil:** Rub it between your fingers to see if it is a sandy, silty or clay soil.
- **Test your soil's acidity or alkalinity:** Buy an easy-to-use kit from your garden centre to check the pH levels of your soil.
- **Choose which vegetables you want:** A good balance between succulent fruits, bulky vegetables and colourful flowers will ensure plenty of variety.
- **Select the right plants:** You may want to avoid ones that take up a lot of space, take a long time to grow or produce poor yields.
- **Make sure you plan your plot carefully:** Try to design a cohesive and logical layout with easy-to-navigate paths and features.
- **Plan an effective crop rotation:** Avoid planting vegetables in exactly the same plot to ensure good harvests and to keep soil-borne pests and diseases at bay.
- **Make sure you choose the right permanent structures:** A good shed, greenhouse and compost bin are important to the smooth running of your allotment.

Preparing to Garden

Tools and Equipment

The vast array of labour-saving equipment in local gardening shops can be quite bewildering to a cautious new arrival on the allotment. The purpose of many tools remains hidden behind their mysterious names – Dutch hoe, rotovator – and forms the strange vocabulary of doing it yourself down on the plot. There is a tool for most jobs, including some you never knew needed doing and some that don't even need doing, so it pays to choose carefully, because the right tool could turn an irksome chore into a pure pleasure.

Tooling Up

Tools can be as expensive as they are desirable, but it may be worth the investment: a good tool can last a lifetime and prove to be good value for money. However, you don't have to

make a beeline for that shiny, polished metal spade gleaming in your garden centre. Check out second-hand shops, online auction sites or car boot sales. Some kit, such as large rotovators, can be hired, while others such as wheelbarrows can be jointly owned by three or four allotment holders.

Marking Up

Look after your tools. Keep them locked away when not in use, and mark them for easy identification. If carving postcodes on to wooden handles lacks the subtle touch, think of using a UV pen or photographing your kit.

Power to the People

Though practice is needed to master the finer points of a few allotment jobs, most tools will bring instant improvement to the products of your labour. But if in doubt how to use that narrow onion hoe, just look at, or ask, how old Fred in the next allotment got his garlic to a tee.

The Full Works

An afternoon of abandon spent amassing the tools of your pleasurable toil can set you back lots of money. All you need to start out are a few basic essentials, then buy selectively as your allotment skills flourish on an array of ever more challenging plants and jobs.

Spade

The spade is the linchpin of a good tool shed and is the key digging instrument. In theory you should use a shovel – a spade with the sides upturned to hold material – to carry soil, but for most of us the spade doubles up as a dirt shifter. You cannot, however, use a shovel to dig. While the spade head can be made from all types of metals, including stainless steel, the handle is the important part. Get the handle height right and it will take lots of strain out of digging.

Top Tip

Check out smaller border spades and see if you prefer T- or D-shaped handgrips.

Fork

The fork comes in all different sizes including the typical mainstay, which is a similar size to a spade and needs the same considerations with handle height and handgrip shape. Border forks are smaller, while smaller still are the hand-held trowels needed for planting and potting up, and hand forks used for weeding. The key quality of a digging fork is strength of tines, so make sure they are made from a single strip of good-quality steel – weak tines will bend when they hit stones.

Rake

The rake is another key tool. This is used to level the soil and achieve a fine surface known as tilth. You can wield it to break down lumpy soil, remove stones or clear scraps of rubbish that have drifted on to your plot. Make sure the shaft and head are well made, and avoid a slapstick but painful bruising of the nose by never laying your fork on the ground teeth up. Someone is bound to tread on it.

Hoe

Another must-have is the hoe and this comes in all shapes and sizes to help you blitz weeds, loosen soil and mark out drills to sow seeds. A Dutch hoe is dragged back and forth to kill weeds, while a looped 'draw hoe' is pulled towards you to chop into weeds. Whatever your hoe, keep it honed using a sharpening stone or file.

Rotovator

These look daunting but are quite easy to use to break up lumpy soil into a finer tilth by mechanical means. Some are lightweight contraptions, while others are walk-behind heavyweights that you can hire or buy new or second hand. Some allotment holders swear by the benefits of rotovation, but a few people insist that they do more harm than good by shredding the roots of perennial weeds and spreading them all over the plot to re-emerge later.

Wheelbarrow

Wheelbarrows are essential for carrying manure, compost and allotment waste such as weeds. They come in all different shapes, sizes and materials, including two-wheeled versions, which are easier to manoeuvre and are a little more stable when heaped full of manure. Their drawback is their clumsiness on narrow paths.

Top Tip

Check recommended tyre pressures and always load two-thirds of the weight towards the front to make the barrow easier to push.

Secateurs

When you start to downsize with tools, such as scissor-like secateurs, remember they are easy to lose. A good rule of thumb is to make sure they are brightly coloured so you can see them easily down on the ground or in a flourishing bed. Brandishing secateurs allows you to prune and cut through plant material, and this is the one tool where it really pays to invest in quality. You may also want to buy a bow saw and lopping shears to trim woody fruit trees or bushes.

Watering Can

The bigger the watering can the heavier it will be when full, but the fewer journeys back and forth to the water butt you'll have to make. Plastic or metal is more an aesthetic choice, though plastic is a little lighter to carry. You will need a fine spray head, which is called a rose, and maybe a smaller watering can for more intricate jobs such as irrigating seedlings.

Mattock

In southern Europe, the mattock – also known by its Spanish name of 'azada' – is a fairly standard tool on the allotment. The broad blunt blade at the end of a robust handle can be used like a draw hoe. It can also be taken out of the shed for clearing big weeds or used like a pickaxe for breaking up concrete-hard soil and removing a big root network. The key safety aspect with mattocks is not to swing it behind your head, but to use small but firm chopping motions from the shoulder down.

Garden Reel and Measuring Stick

The garden reel can be strung out from top to bottom of a bed to ensure a super-straight drill for sowing your seeds. A measuring stick can be bought from a garden centre or made from a length of wood with marks or notches every 15 cm (6 in) or so, which you use as a spacing tool for laying seeds in soil.

Toolbox

It's never a bad idea to have a toolbox tucked away in your allotment shed for those nagging repair jobs on the fence or trellis. A claw hammer will enable you to knock in nails and claw them out again, a panel saw will make short work of cutting planks and a hacksaw will cut through thin wooden strips or bamboo.

Looking After Your Tools

Look after your tools and they will look after you. Always keep a box of cleaning, care and repair gear in your allotment shed, packed with rags, brushes, wire wool, files, a sharpening stone and a can of lubricating oil. The latter should be used on tools with moving parts such as secateurs or shears to keep them rust free and working smoothly. Spades and forks should be wiped clear of mud and given a really good cleaning every month or so.

Safety

Many allotment gardeners store their tools in a corner of the garden shed, which is fine until a child ambles by. Dark, out-of-sight places like these are irresistible to children, so it's a good idea to keep tools with blades, edges and points locked away. If you hang up your forks and rakes on pegs, make sure the tines face the walls and hosepipes can be safely coiled on wall-mounted frames or on cassette reels.

Soil Improvement

A rich, healthy soil is vital. The essence of improving the soil is to create a balanced loam, which means making overlight soils heavier and heavier soils lighter. In both cases, the main agent for improving soil structure is called humus. This is a storehouse of nutrients, which coats sand and silt to make them crumbly. Fortunately, the very act of cultivating fruit, vegetables and flowers on your plot can help the fertility of the soil. But there are other ways to bump up productivity like using compost and fertilizer.

Compost Convert

An allotment without compost is as useful as a boat without a paddle – both shortcomings will leave you floundering. Fortunately, commercial compost can be bought by the bagful from any garden centre. Though plants can not only grow but thrive in ordinary allotment soil, compost offers them a few nutritious goodies to give them a flying start. There are different kinds of composts, including:

- **Seed compost**: This is low in nutrients, has a fine texture and usually contains peat or a peat substitute.
- **Potting compost**: You can also use this for propagating cuttings; it drains well to make waterlogged roots less likely.
- **General-purpose compost**: A good all-rounder, this should contain all the nutrients to encourage healthy plant growth.

Spread It About

The amount of compost you need on your plot will vary depending on the condition of your soil, size of allotment bed and what you want to grow. About two or three bucketfuls per square metre should be an ample amount, worked into the soil thoroughly and evenly annually.

Do It Yourself

You don't have to buy your compost in large 70 litre (18 gallon) bags. Compost – or rather the act of composting – is all around us, from the decaying fallen leaves in autumn to the rotting fruit in your bowl. The best compost is a healthy mixture of organic materials, from soft, green grass clippings, fruit peelings and unwanted vegetables to woody hedge trimmings and other oddments such as cardboard and eggshells. This is a form of compost that doesn't cost a penny. You can make it yourself.

Did You Know?

Compost typically contains a balanced mix of nitrogen (N), phosphorus (P), potassium (K) and other nutrients that benefit plants.

What Rot!

DIY composting is a perfect way of recycling all your allotment plant debris and also some of your household waste. You are thereby putting back into the soil some of what you've taken out. The first thing you will need is not one but two compost bins or structures made out of pallets. This will enable you to fill one of the bins while the contents of the other are rotting down.

Compost Cocktail

The trick of blending good compost is to make sure you are piling together a healthy mixture of materials. Too much green waste such as grass cuttings, dead weeds and leafy stems will turn into a stinky, slimy sludge, yet if all your compost is made up of only brown, woody material like prunings from your fruit trees, it might not break down at all. Mix brown and green together and you have the perfect cocktail for your cabbages and cucumbers.

Be Consistent

What you are trying to achieve with your compost is an even consistency: not too dry, not too wet and not too compacted. You may have to damp down the heap in summer and add scrunched-up brown paper in the winter if your heap becomes too watery. But when the conditions are right, nitrogen-rich materials increase the temperature in the heap and speed up decomposition. Some allotment holders insulate their bins with cardboard to increase the temperature. A vigorous forking from time to time will ensure plenty of air circulation and healthy compost for your soil in a year's time.

No Entry

Some things should never go together, so do not compost perennial weed roots, diseased or pest-ridden plants and cat or dog faeces.

Surface Meaning

The word 'compost' comes from the Latin word 'compositus', which means put together.

Fertile Ground

Chemical-based fertilizers, which offer more concentrated forms of inorganic food like nitrogen and phosphates, are widely available to the allotment holder, and offer plants quick bursts of nutrition. This can give a real boost to vegetables such as brassicas, big feeders that love nothing more than a nitrogen-rich fix. But take care: overapplying fertilizer can leave plants sappy, while salts from the feed can build up in the soil over years, forcing worms and other salt-hating micro-organisms to seek pastures new.

Off the Hoof

Organic fertilizer, such as phosphate-rich bone meal, and hoof and horn, a slow-release source of nitrogen, can also be applied on the allotment. This form of feeding is fast and simple — sprinkle the granules around the crops any time throughout the growing season. Some allotment gardeners say well-rotted manure does the trick of a fertilizer, but take note, the nutrient levels are lower and best used for improving the soil.

Read the Labels

Get into the habit of reading the instructions on feed packets. A quick glance at the 'NPK ratios' will give you an idea of the amounts of nitrogen (N), phosphorus (P) and potassium (K), information that you will need if you are comparing fertilizers. Some terms commonly used on the allotment are:

Balanced fertilizer: Contains roughly equal amounts of nitrogen, phosphorus and potassium.

 Base dressing: Fertilizer you can rake into the ground before planting.

 Top dressing: Fertilizer spread on top of the soil and around established crops.

No Animals

In addition to the organic fertilizers, the allotment holder has a tantalizing array of non-animal material and soil conditioners. Seaweed meal should be applied three months before planting, contains minor nutrients and helps bind together sands and clays. Lime, not a fertilizer in itself, raises pH levels (*see* page 54), while rock dust is a by-product from quarrying that contains many trace elements and is good for sandy soils. This last one improves water retention and soil fertility.

Breathe Carefully

Fertilizers are spread on to the soil as granular pellets, as fine dry powder or as a liquid mixed with water. Always take care when using dusty fertilizers such as bone meal and avoid breathing in the powder. You should also wear gloves and don't forget to wash your hands afterwards.

How Much to Use?

Few allotment gardeners have the luxury of enough space in their sheds to accommodate scales, though maybe a few of you could chip in together. For some new plot holders, reading '300 g per sq m' on the back of a fertilizer packet will be all but meaningless. So: 100 g (3½ oz) is about enough granules to fill a small jar or yogurt pot.

Seeds and Plants

Pick up a seed catalogue, any one will do, or pluck any seed packet off a shelf at a local garden centre and look at the images of stunning blooms and vegetables bursting with colour and ripeness. In the allotment garden, everything is usually started with seed with a few exceptions such as artichokes, generally grown from tubers or root suckers. It's not hard to see why when you look at all that potential locked up in a seed. What starts as a tiny dot sown in the chills of March could be a 2 m (7 ft) high tomato plant six months later.

Times Change

Nurturing plants from seed is held dear by plot holders, although this way is tricky and takes time. Fortunately, choices on the allotment have increased in more ways than the range of exotic vegetables that can be cultivated. Allotment gardeners can now grow from small plants, called plug plants (see page 96), though seeds will always hold a special place in the hearts and minds of many plot holders.

Seed Banks

Seeds need tender loving care and need the best possible growing conditions, including the right temperature, moisture and light levels, so it pays to read the growing instructions on the back of the pack. Then read them again for good measure. Many things can thwart those seeds, from slugs to bad weather.

North-South Divide

Growing conditions may vary in different geographic locations. What grows well in southern regions or countries will not always thrive so well in harsher northern climates. This is where forging good friendships with neighbouring, more experienced plot holders on the site will help. They can give you an idea of which types of seeds do well in your area.

Look Out

While sowing seeds is good fun and fairly easy, there are a few things you need to look out for:

- Try to follow the instructions on when to sow and harvest, but don't worry too much if you are a little out on timing – seed is small, but fairly robust.
- Some crops are best sown in seed beds and later moved, or transplanted, to their final growing spot.
- If you have very small children on the plot, they may have difficulties with tiny seed, so choose larger seed for them to plant, such as sweetcorn or runner beans.
- Most seeds won't last more than a few years at the most, so make sure you use or give away seed before its expiry date.

Testing Seeds

If you find an old packet of seeds in your shed drawer you can test to see if the contents will germinate by sprinkling a dozen or so seeds on to a damp piece of blotting paper or kitchen paper and placing it all in a plastic bag. If fewer than half germinate, treat the pack with suspicion.

Seeds of All Shapes

Seeds come in many forms, from bulky runner beans to smaller pellet-like carrots. Seed that can be prodded or dribbled into the ground from your hand includes broad beans, spring onions and beetroot. Minuscule celery seed is almost like powder, while cucumber is as flat and long as parsnip seed is round and small.

All Shapes, All Sizes

As well as planting seeds in a row you can push like onion sets (small bulbs) into the earth so the tip just pokes above the soil, or you can drop potato seeds into large holes or into a wide drill and cover them.

The Good News

Growing from seed involves inspiration and a fair measure of trial and error, but it has many advantages, including cheapness. You know exactly what varieties you are getting and, some will argue, you avoid the risk of using in a plant that may be diseased.

The Not So Good News

The trouble with growing from seed is unless you are careful you can end up with too many vegetables. Each seed packet usually contains enough seeds for several gardeners and it is not unknown for plot holders to end up with hundreds of seedlings of one vegetable. This represents something of a catch-22 – seeds do not last indefinitely, so the temptation is to plant in large volumes, and growing seeds eats into your time – the one thing some allotment holders do not have on their hands.

Plug the Gap

Seed companies, latching on to the need – or desire – for allotment holders to streamline workloads, have been only too pleased to oblige in recent years. Buying young plants that are still in 'plug' form can be a fast and cost-effective way of raising plants. The mini courgettes and strawberries are simply removed from their casing and plugged straight into the prepared allotment bed.

Plug plants are seedlings that have been germinated and grown in trays. When the roots are big enough they can be removed from the trays and transplanted into larger pots or put straight outside in the allotment. Once they were a luxury confined to lovers of bedding plants, but all that changed with the growing popularity of edible gardening, spearheaded by allotment holders, of course.

Hitching on the Bandwagon

Many nurseries and seed companies now sell a range of fruit and vegetable plug plants such as cabbage, cauliflower and lettuce. These offer a fairly easy route to starting a productive allotment, their main advantage being that roots stay undisturbed when transplanting them into their final growing position: even experienced plot holders lose soil from the roots when lifting seedlings.

Put a Plug In It

Plugs can be good for allotment holders starting out with vegetables: it is easy to miss the correct sowing times when you are new to growing, while seeds need to be ordered early.

How Do I Plant My Plug Plants?

Smaller plugs prefer being potted in slightly larger containers for two to three weeks before going into your plot, but larger-sized plugs can be planted straight out in the allotment after their rootballs have been given a good watering and left to 'rest' for a day or so.

Before planting them out you should ensure the plants are well watered. Remove them from their trays by prodding the bottom of the container with your finger, then with your finger or a pencil, prod a neat little hole in the compost and drop the plant into the hole.

Carefully Does It

Using plug plants cuts out the hassle of sowing and pricking out. They are fairly dependable but fragile, so it's worth treading carefully to start with. Keep the plug tray in a light, frost-free place away from the wind. That cosy nook by your shed window, or the lower shelf in the greenhouse, looks an ideal spot, but don't forget to water them gently.

Plugging Plants

Plug plant converts argue that raising young seedlings inside is time consuming and too easy to get wrong and therefore stunt the plants. Seed stalwarts say small plug plants are fiddly and take out all the pleasure of creating life from seed and watching that first green shoot grow to full maturity. Like so many things down on the allotment, it's all down to taste.

Clearing the Plot

Looking – or wincing – at your allotment plot for the first time can be a sobering experience that makes you want to reach for the hard stuff. It is unlikely to be the neatly manicured plot next to the communal tap you had your eye on, but it could be the wasteland in the far corner you mistook at first glance for a giant compost heap. Sometimes the new allotment holder will behold a site almost carpeted in brambles and nettles. Other times they turn up trumps with a plot in fair condition; good luck.

Third Degree Neglect

If you are lucky, the damage will be superficial and little more than annual weeds. These are fairly easy to deal with and a few bumps in the ground that can be raked smooth in no time. Even if your plot is an overgrown mess, fear not. It can still be turned into a productive piece of land.

What Do You Want?

Why make life hard for yourself? The plot may be little more than a jungle of writhing undergrowth, but some of that botanic tangle and jumble of odds and ends might be worth keeping, so note any plants or features you want to retain: maybe a straggling blackberry bush needs only a trim; perhaps that shed could do with a few more panels to make it perfectly workable.

What Don't You Want?

Take a close look at the things you do not want on your plot. Make a note of all those things you need to banish, and do just that, but not yet. The weeds in your plot will give you a clue to the soil conditions you will have to work with, so it makes sense to look before leaping in with a scythe or strimmer.

Use Your Indicators

Weeds that give you an idea of the type of soil on your allotment include:

- **Clover:** The allotment ground is possibly low in nitrogen content.
- **Dock:** This weed is giving you a hint your soil is probably acidic.
- **Couch grass and creeping buttercup:** These both suggest your earth is compacted.
- **Horsetail:** You are more likely to have damp and heavy clay soil.
- **Sow thistle and wild mustard:** These are indicator weeds for alkaline soils.

What's a Weed?

Weeds are simply plants that you don't want growing on your plot but have adapted well to the soil and conditions in your area.

Weeding Out the Weeds

When it comes to dealing with plants, wanted or otherwise, the saying 'one year's seeding gives seven years' weeding' rings only too true. You must be thorough in your weeding and whatever type of hoe you use, keep it sharp so that the tops of weeds are cut off cleanly.

Perennial Problems

Having decided what to keep and what to jettison after gleaning all the telltale information on your soil, it helps to know your enemy. Weeds, like other plants, fall into three categories: annuals, biennials and perennials.

Annual Weeds

Annual weeds like groundsel and chickweed are the easiest to blitz, but have a nasty tendency to come back. These plants germinate, grow and then die in one season, but not before scattering copious amounts of seed that will grow back next year. They have shallow root systems that penetrate no lower than the topsoil, making them easy to remove by hoeing or plucking them out by hand one by one. Get in there early, though, because if annual weeds take hold they come back year after year and it can be hard to keep on top of the problem. You don't want your annuals to become a perennial problem.

Biennial Weeds

Biennial weeds take two seasons to grow and die. A long taproot is topped with a few leaves above the soil surface in the first season. In the second season comes the fall-out from a stem and flower, which drops hundreds of seeds. These are best dealt with by gently uprooting, ideally before the flower and stem have grown.

Perennial Weeds

Perennial weeds are the real 'baddies' of your allotment and include couch grass, dock, ground elder and nettles. They are persistent thorns in the sides of plot holders and come back year after year thanks to a tenacious network of roots. All of this root system must be totally removed or killed if you are to see the back of the weed for good. Some, like dock, are easier to deal with: just lever a fork into the ground when the soil is moist and ease out the weed with a gentle tug. Couch and ground elder are much harder to tackle and some allotment holders resort to weedkiller. Others try to suppress the weeds by covering the ground with polythene (*see* page 103).

Jungle Warfare

Getting started on your allotment is likely to be action-packed and involve an armoury of tools, including a strimmer – hired, borrowed or bought – a scythe and maybe loppers and shears. The objective is simple, the job less so. You have to wade into the undergrowth and fell it. Once everything has been levelled you will be able to see the shape and size of land you will be dealing with in the coming months.

Going Underground

Once you have lopped all the weeds back to ground level, you have to attack their roots. Brace yourself for some hard graft, as many perennials have large root systems that anchor themselves deep into the soil. Most also have the ability to regenerate themselves and grow from the tiniest section of underground stem, called a rhizome. This is why it is important – but almost impossible – to eradicate the entire root system. Many of these weeds can defy even weedkiller so it's back to the good old spade. Most allotment holders resign themselves to a long war of attrition, which involves digging out the weeds and digging them out again when they reappear a few weeks later.

Top Tip

Don't worry about the mountain of debris: leaving it in the sun to dry will make it shrink as moisture evaporates, or you can cover it all with a tarpaulin; but only when all the weeds are dead should you consign them to the compost heap.

Perennial Problem

Perennial weeds are a downer but not a disaster; as long as you keep digging them out and don't let them overrun the plot, you can still make the most of your allotment's productivity.

Round and Round

Some allotment holders like to use what looks like a mini plough to break up the soil surface into a fine tilth. You can hire rotovators (*see* page 85) from mower specialists or buy small lightweight versions, and the narrower the tines the easier it will be to move around the plot. This could be an important thing to consider if your site is very uneven.

Fire It Up

Rotovators can save a lot of backbreaking work in the early stages of preparing a plot but are not a total alternative to digging. The machines can struggle on heavy clay soils and,

unless you have sifted all the weed roots out of the earth, the spinning tines will simply chop them into finer fragments and churn them around the plot. This will almost certainly make your weed problem a good deal worse.

Cover Up

There is a third way of dealing with weeds. If you don't want to dig them up with a fork, and if you can't pluck up the courage to rumble into action with a rotovator, you can simply cover your ground elder and dock with a tarpaulin, old carpet, black polythene or even cardboard. This will starve the weeds of light and should kill them over a year or two. You will need to dig the corners of the fabric into the earth or weigh them down with bricks, and the whole visual spectacle of covering weeds is not pretty.

However, this is a quick way of dealing with a time-consuming problem and does not have to be an all-or-nothing remedy to weeds. You can cover half your site with polythene, leaving you to concentrate your time and efforts on clearing and cultivating half a plot for the next year or so. Covering your soil has the added benefit of keeping moisture in its place, down below.

Like the Carpet

Check allotment rules on using old carpets to block out weeds. Some don't allow it because worn shagpile rarely leaves the plot when its owner calls it a day for the last time, leaving the association with a bulky disposal problem. Artificial carpet may also be deemed unbiodegradable. It can leave small bits of foam in the soil, and some people think that chemicals from dyes can leak into the earth.

Dress Up

Clearing an allotment is a messy business and you should dress for the occasion. Tough boots and gloves are a must, and some allotment holders even don protective goggles when wading into thorny or high weeds. There are other things to look out for when trawling through dense undergrowth, including broken glass. Asbestos sheets, often used for shed panels, jagged, makeshift fencing and hazardous chemicals left in bottles have also turned up on allotment sites.

Staggered Start

As you clear the plot, think of your overall allotment plan. It may be possible to plant as you progress, and don't worry about the weeds that continually poke their head above the parapet. Pluck them out or hoe them down. Clearing your plot is one of the hardest jobs you will undertake on your allotment, but the results are rewarding.

Preparing the Soil

Whatever your soil, the chances are you'll always want to improve it. As well as composts and fertilizers there are other ways of giving your soil the best possible start when you are preparing your allotment. For some plot holders this means digging. Love it or hate it, digging is seen by these growers as terrific for opening up compacted soil, aerating it and creating the conditions for you to enrich it.

Dirty Work

You can use the spade in many ways, with single or double digging and trenching being held especially dear by the dirt diggers. Though heaving up the earth is time consuming and strenuous, this die-hard breed insists with one voice that digging brings you into closer contact with the soil than any other allotment activity and tells you a lot about the quality of the earth.

How to Make Digging Easier

Mark out a clod of soil with three vertical cuts of the spade and slip the spade into the earth with the fourth cut. At the same time, slide your hand down the length of the handle towards the base to make lifting easier and put less strain on your muscles. Lift and turn the soil over on itself, rest, repeat, rest, repeat, rest, repeat...

Double Digging

Double digging is perhaps the best-known way of excavating an allotment with a spade and means cultivating the soil to a depth of two spade heads. It is a good way of treating a new plot or shaking up a sluggishly heavy and compacted soil.

How to Double Dig

First, divide your plot down the middle lengthways and then:

 Starting on one corner, dig a trench about 30 cm (1 ft) wide and remove the topsoil to the depth of one spade and pile it on one side.

 Add manure or compost to the bottom of the trench and turn it over to the full depth of a fork to blend the material into the subsoil.

 Dig another trench next to the first one but throw the topsoil into the first trench you dug, and continue repeating this process trench after trench.

- Once you have covered the site, digging and filling trenches, you will come to the final ditch. This you should fill with the topsoil you put to one side after digging the first trench.
- Many allotment gardeners say as long as your plot soil is waterlogged, compacted or lacking in organic nutrients, you should dig. If, however, you have sandy, silty or other soils with better structure and balance there may be little point taking such drastic action as double digging.

Mulch Culture

Double digging is quite a heavy-handed way of tackling a leaden soil structure and could upset the delicate microcosm under the surface. A more deft treatment may be to add organic materials by mulching. Mulches are layers of organic or inorganic matter that blanket the soil to keep out weeds and lock in moisture. These include the usual suspects such as plastic sheeting and carpet as well as chipped bark or straw.

More Mulches

Mulches offer other benefits: they help improve soil structure, cut the risk of soil erosion and compaction, and regulate the temperature of the earth by retaining warmth in autumn and protecting from frost later in the year. If you use an organic mulch such as manure, it will feed the soil as it decays on the surface. Inorganic materials, while offering no nutritional benefit to the soil, can nevertheless last for several seasons – if you can put up with the ugliness of polythene or the brash but unwanted 1970s kitchen lino.

When's a Good Time?

There's no time like the present is a good adage on the allotment, but sometimes it doesn't work that way. Mulch is best laid when the soil is reasonably warm. Mulch too early and you can lock in that coldness underground. Early spring is a good time to apply cover, when the earth still contains moisture from the winter rains.

What Lies Beneath

Taking the long view of your soil may be your only option. The ground beneath your feet is more than likely a swampy composition that has accumulated from use by several generations of allotment holders. Some of them would have been on compost overdrive, others would have relied on the quick fix of fertilizers. Put organic matter on soil and it is turned to humus. This dark crumbly material is great for your soil, encouraging water retention, aeration and strong roots. The darker your soil the more humus it contains, while pale soil suggests your plot has been starved of organic matter. There are several ways of boosting the amount of matter in your soil than with compost or a quick shot in the form of fertilizer.

Muck About

Manure is a big favourite on the allotment, but not everyone on the allotment favours manure. Piles of steaming dung are probably out if you're a vegan, while some organic allotment growers frown on manure from animals reared on intensively farmed landholdings. Other growers prefer to sidestep manure because it can be chock-full of weed seeds. An alternative source of manure if you live in an urban area could be a city farm, run less intensively than bigger farms.

Heap Thrills

There are many alternatives to the bags of compost and soil improvers that you can turn to when looking to improve your soil. Other choices include:

- **Leaf mould:** Make this yourself by bagging up fallen leaves and leaving them to decay for about a year. You can dig them into the soil or use as a mulch to help the soil retain its moisture and repel weeds. Leaves take a long time to rot down but make a great soil conditioner by improving its structure. Leaf mould is light, crumbly and packed with carbon.

- **Worm compost:** Check out worm composting kits and the time and effort needed to run a wormery, a plastic dining room for worms feeding off your kitchen waste. Each one processes your potato peelings and browning banana skins into a material that is fantastic for your allotment's soil. Most wormeries are made of a stack of trays, into which you feed your kitchen waste from the top.

Green manure: Green manures are usually from the legume family and are grown for one season before being dug back into the soil to enrich it for the crops you want to nurture. Growing a green manure crop is good because it provides ground cover and suppresses weeds. Its roots break up the earth and improve soil structure. Green manures include grazing rye and buckwheat.

Liquid Diet

If organic or inorganic fertilizers are not enough, the plot holder has another ace for preparing the ground in readiness for his fruit, vegetables and flowers. They can fill up with liquid plant manure, which is easy to make, costs virtually nothing and boasts a fair amount of effectiveness, but brace yourself: liquid plant manures stink to high heaven. One of the most popular is comfrey manure.

Brew Up

To make comfrey manure, you need to throw plenty of leaves into a sack and place it in a water butt, clamping the lid firmly shut to keep away the smell. The potash-rich slurry that emerges about a month later is bad on the nose but good on tomatoes, potatoes, berries and onions. You can also use borage liquid manure, which is nitrogen rich, and its nettle equivalent.

Top Tip

When handling comfrey it's a good idea to wear gloves as the plant leaves have hairs that irritate some gardeners.

How Much Do I Need?

The quantities you will need to give your allotment a reasonable drenching are around 1 kg (2 lb 4 oz) of comfrey, borage or nettle leaves and 10 litres (18 pints) of water. Pour the manure on to your soil in a mixture of one part manure to 10 parts water.

Checklist

- **Get the right tools**: Choosing well will save money in the long run and make your job easier.
- **Make sure your soil is rich and healthy**: This is the key to success on the allotment.
- **The amount of compost you need varies**: It depends on the condition of your soil, size of the allotment bed and what you want to grow.
- **Fertilizers offer plants quick bursts of nutrition**: This can give a real boost to flagging fruit, vegetables and flowers.
- **Seeds or plugs**: Allotment holders can grow from traditional seed or buy mini 'plug' plants to avoid having to sow from scratch.
- **Plugs are growing in popularity**: Many nurseries and seed companies now sell a wide range of produce including strawberries, cabbages, cauliflowers and lettuce.
- **Clearing a plot is one of the hardest jobs**: It is also one of the most rewarding, giving you a glimpse of the challenge ahead.
- **There are many alternatives to compost**: These include green manure, leaf mould and worm compost.

Gardening
Time

When and How to Sow

Seed is something no allotment gardener can be without, and sowing seed can be one of the easiest jobs on the plot, as well as one of the most time consuming and rewarding. Even the most hardened and experienced allotment gardener enjoys an epiphany-type moment each season when the seed planted a few weeks ago shows the first signs of life with those first green shoots.

Right Conditions

All seeds need warmth, moisture and air to germinate, so when to sow your seeds will depend on soil temperature and hardiness. Some of the more hardy plants such as early carrots and maincrop broad beans can be sown outdoors from February, others including sprouting broccoli, could do with being held back until April or May.

Preparing the Ground

Before sowing, you need to prepare the beds. Clear the soil of weeds and stones and rake it into a fine tilth. The golden rule is the smaller the seed, the finer the tilth but, for most medium-size to large seed, soil the texture of breadcrumbs works a treat.

Get Sowing

The commonest and easiest way of sowing seed is outside and directly into the soil. Most seed on the allotment can be grown this way, but keep an eye on the thermometer. You need to wait until the soil is warm enough for the seeds to germinate. Cold snaps or extended chilly weather can delay your harvest at best and wipe it out at worst.

Don't Get Stitched Up

You should always buy the best-quality seeds to minimize the chance of a disappointing harvest. Other ways to improve your chances of a bumper harvest from your sown seed are to:

- Store your seeds in a cool place; heat can damage the germinating properties of the seed and affect or destroy growth.
- If you store seeds in your allotment shed, make sure the container you use is firmly sealed and airtight to keep out moisture and mice.

Sowing Some Happiness

Sowing seeds takes patience but the job itself is reassuringly straightforward. You need little more than a piece of string, two canes, a stick, seeds and the land you have prepared so lovingly. This is how you sow seeds:

- Tie the string to the two canes stuck at either end of the well-prepared, raked bed you have chosen to plant.
- Use the end of a stick to make a narrow v-shaped trench in the soil beside the string stretched in a line across the ground.
- Lightly water the bottom of the trench, which should be around 4 cm (1½ in) deep for large seeds such as beans and half as deep for small seeds like beetroot.
- Place the seeds in the bottom of the trench with your fingers or tap them out of the seed packet or your hand to distribute them evenly along the trench.

Fill in the soil from the trench and firm it gently with your hand or the head of a rake – growing in a straight line makes it easy to spot out-of-sync weeds a few weeks later.

Taking to the Air

You can also 'broadcast' seed for some herbs and salad leaf crops. Walk up and down the bed scattering seed in a wide arc but as evenly as possible, rake over the soil gently and water.

Depth and Spacing

It is a good idea to glean planting details from the seed packet or ask a fellow allotment holder. Generally, the soil you cover the seed with should be no deeper than the seed's diameter. The smaller the seed, the shallower the drill and the thinner the coverage of soil it will need. With spacing, think of the hopeful size of the end product. Cucumber and marrow seed, for example, need to be spaced at about 60 cm (2 ft).

Top Tip

All seed should be sown thinly because overcrowded seedlings quickly become weak and are more likely to be attacked by disease.

Protecting Newly Planted Seeds and Plants

Cold weather and wild animals can destroy all the fruits of your labour, so you need to protect against the former and keep out the latter, if possible. Fortunately, you have plenty of allies to hand in the form of cloches, coldframes, mini polytunnels, horticultural fleece and netting.

Protection Racket

The main point of protection is to increase the amount of growing time for your plants and there is no doubt a little protection of some kind, however makeshift, pays dividends on the allotment. It:

- Raises the soil and air temperature to extend the growing season and the range of crops.
- Ensures borderline crops such as tomatoes can be grown successfully whatever the season.
- Shields crops against the elements to help you increase yields and productivity.
- Provides shelter from frost and combats the killer combination of cold winds and low temperatures.
- Reduces damage from birds, which can cause massive problems: pigeons adore plundering winter greens.

Undercover Operations

✅ **Coldframes:** One of the best ways of acclimatizing seedlings and more tender fare on the allotment, such as aubergines, is to grow them in a small enclosure with a glass roof called a coldframe. Place seedlings in the coldframe a few weeks before you want to plant them out to 'harden them off' and give them a taster of what's in store for them.

✅ **Cloches and mini polytunnels:** Glass, clear rigid plastic or heavy-duty polythene can be used to cover plants in beds, while large plastic bottles cut in half also make good protection for individual plants: use the top half with the lid removed to shelter the plant. Mini polytunnels can be made by stretching clear polythene over metal hoops to cover the bed.

✅ **Horticultural fleece and netting:** Fleece is a breathable blanket you cover your crops with, which lets in moisture, light and air. As well as protection from cold weather, it is also good at keeping away flying pests, rabbits and mice. Netting or wire mesh are more traditional ways of protecting your plants from large pests, such as birds.

Make Your Own

Small structures throw open big opportunities for thrifty allotment holders. Why not knock up a simple A-frame structure out of two old windows leant into each other like an old ridge tent and secured with pegs and rope? A cover like this costs nothing to make and is perfect for protecting your seedlings.

Greenhouses

Stepping up a size takes you into the greenhouse, a haven of warmth and protection for your seedlings and young plants and somewhere to overwinter tender fruits and vegetables. You need to control the conditions carefully to ensure plants do not become too moist or too dry. There are lots of models, so look at them and ask your allotment neighbours which ones they favour – and why. Check if the allotment landlord allows a greenhouse on the plot.

Wind Shelter

Ever wondered what to do with that old sheet of see-through corrugated plastic in the corner of your allotment shed? Prop it up between wooden posts at either end of the plastic and you have a highly effective mini windbreak.

Top Tip

Before buying a greenhouse or making a glazed cloche, find out if pests in the form of vandals prey on your site: plastic may save you a few shattered dreams.

Material Possessions

The sort of protection you choose will depend on the size of the allotment, its orientation and the crops you grow. Should you go for permanence in the form of a greenhouse, or a semi-permanent shelter like a polythene-clad structure? Glass transmits light best, retains more heat at night and does not deteriorate with age. However, it is expensive, heavy to build and there are bound to be breakages.

Plastic materials are cheaper and lighter but lose heat more quickly at night. Whatever you choose, anchor your protective systems against wind damage, close the end of cloches to avoid a wind tunnel effect and mend tears in synthetic material immediately.

Transplanting Seedlings

As soon as your seedlings have hardened off under the cloche or in the warmth of the greenhouse they are ready to be moved to the plot. Lifting fragile seedlings and planting them in their final growing space is a delicate task and should be done after about two weeks to a month of growing under cover.

Minimize Risk

A good time to transplant is after you've seen the worst of the frost. To minimize this cold shock, prepare the bed that will be the plants' new home into a fine, stone-free tilth. Make holes with a 'dibber', pencil or finger big enough to take the seedling and all of its rootball — no roots should be seen above the soil when the plant has gone to ground.

Pricking Out and Potting On

Water both soil and seedling before lifting them, but be gentle. When you start transplanting, remember to work quickly but efficiently especially when handling the plant. Pick it up by the leaves and not the stem, which is delicate and easy to break. Ease the seedling out with the dibber and move to the new pot or bed. To pot on to a larger container, put one hand over the top of the smaller pot with a finger either side of the seedling stem. Turn the pot upside down and gently lift the pot off the rootball.

Root It Out

Try to take all or as much of the soil around the rootball as possible and plant in the bed at the same level it was in the small pot or tray from which it came. Firm the soil around it but try to avoid pressing too hard or you will compact the earth. Don't forget to water the plant as soon as you have finished transplanting. Even if you are working in a drizzle or light rain, watering will ensure soil wraps around the roots like a perfect-fitting glove.

Give Your Trans-plants the Best Chance

- **Room to grow**: When you transplant, try to ensure uniformity by using a measuring stick and a line so that your rows are straight and the plants evenly spaced.
- **Keeping cool**: In still, baking-hot summers it's a good idea to give your newly transplanted seedlings a little shade with newspaper propped up tent-like on a frame made of sticks.
- **Quenching thirst**: Once the plants are settled in, continue to water and scatter some organic mulch around each stem to prevent water loss from the roots.

How Often to Allotment?

Working on an allotment is multitasking writ large: no two jobs are the same and no two days are the same. This makes plotting how much time you will have to dedicate to your beetroot and artichokes tough to gauge. A couple of hours a week may see you through the 'quiet season' in the winter months, but by early spring you will need to think about setting aside more time for sowing seeds and planting seedlings, and then it gets really busy.

Watch the Clock

As well as sowing and planting, there will be weeding to do followed by watering, so you may need to spend around 15 hours a week on the plot. Harvesting, which takes place from June onwards, will swallow up time, especially if you have staggered your crop planting to avoid a glut. However you structure your visits – half hourly, daily, per weekend – you need to put in an appearance at least once a week just to keep on top of weeds and pests. The more complex the plot, the more time you will probably have to spend keeping it in line.

Top Tip

Allotment holders should consider the equivalent of half an hour's work each day on their plot as a minimum time to achieve reasonable results, according to the UK's National Society of Allotment and Leisure Gardeners.

Good Housekeeping

Following a regular routine with your visits – set days and evenings every week – should make it easier to allocate ongoing tasks on the plot and help you to plan start and finish dates.

Taking a more scatter-gun approach of squeezing in visits when you can, or not at all when time is tight, can see you fall behind on sowing, planting and tidying up jobs. And there lies disaster, for growing seasons are tight and a measure of good housekeeping on the plot is important to hit all those deadlines.

Make Records

As well as timetabling a routine for visiting your allotment, it pays to develop a system of record keeping, which will help save you time and make the most of each visit you make. This can help you to:

- Remember what times in the year pests such as gooseberry mildew attack, so you can plot an advance action plan.
- Make a note of the success or failure of particular crops or varieties – some plot holders log harvesting dates and weight of crops picked.
- Keep track of problems such as growing conditions that may affect only certain parts of the plot.
- Record your many successes and tweaks to planting regimes, such as changing usual sowing patterns or planting a crop later than usual.

Support

Some of your fruit, vegetables and flowers will be rigorous growers and self-clinging climbers. They will therefore need some form of support, and this could involve a frame of over 2 m (6½ ft). Whenever you plant tall crops such as runner beans or blackberries, bear in mind they will need some kind of structure, be it post and wire or bamboo wigwam, to give them a helping hand.

Watch the Wind

The first time you think of growing a tall plant on your plot, your second thought should be what is the direction of the prevailing wind? Avoid planting rows of crops facing the incoming gusts, as every plant will receive a buffeting, which will make for a poorer harvest. Your pride and joy of a structure, meanwhile, is more likely to collapse.

Into the Wind

A safer option for your plants and your handiwork is to plant your rows of raspberries and beans in the direction of the wind, so it receives the minimum resistance. This will expose only the end of each row of crop nearest to the oncoming wind to its force. If your chosen plants are annual, such as runner beans and sweet peas, your structure can be a fairly lightweight affair, made of bamboo pushed into the ground. Permanent crops, such as fruit, will need much sturdier support such as wooden posts and wires.

Top Tip

One of the sturdiest and most attractive structures for the climbing beans on your plot is a wigwam of bamboo, which can take strong winds from any direction.

Typical Supports

Making supports for your allotment allows you to throw a little creativity into the mix. Though the frame you train your fruit and climbing vegetable plants off must be sturdy, you can indulge in all manner of sculptural forms to create a support that catches the eye and does the job to a tee.

Get In Frame

Typical supports you could use include:

 Bean supports: One of the most effective supports takes the form of a row of criss-crossed bamboo sticks, tied where they cross at the top and secured with a horizontal pole. On exposed allotments this bipod-type structure can be bolstered with bigger stakes driven into the ground alongside every other leaning pole.

 Raspberries or blackberries: A good support for training fruit such as blackberries is a post-and-wire structure called a stool system. New leafy canes are trained through a double wire strung up between two posts. Spread the new fruit canes in a fan shape to catch the sun and allow the air to circulate, then bend them over a third wire secured at the top of the two posts.

Watering

Water is the basis of all existence and routine is an important part of life. The trick to irrigating plants on your allotment is to fall into a regular pattern. Plants are creatures of habit, but sadly keeping everything well watered on an allotment is one of the hardest jobs you can undertake. The amount you have to water will depend on your soil and local climate, the kind of plants you are growing and the seasons.

Thirsty Work

Watering is a time- and energy-consuming chore, so it helps to make sure you are efficient at watering. Different allotments have different rules on water – some have taps, others rely on metered supplies. Some draw water from pumps and wells, others ban the use of hosepipes,

which is not hard to understand – hosepipes can spray a massive 900 litres (198 gallons) of water an hour. If you can use a hose, it may be less water consuming to fill up your butt and draw the water with a watering can.

When to Splash

The best time to water is early morning or early evening, especially in summer, to avoid evaporation of the water and to prevent wet leaves from scorching in the sun. Try not to water later in the evening, as plants left too moist overnight are a magnet for slugs and fungal diseases.

Well Watered

A key to good watering is never to water when it is not needed. Overwatering can be as bad as starving your plants of moisture.

Don't Overdo It

Excessive watering can:

- Wash nutrients and nitrogenous fertilizer below the root zone.
- Discourage root growth and make plants more susceptible to drought.
- Increase the growth of the plant without increasing the edible part.
- Saturate the plant tissue and make the plant more susceptible to disease.
- Worst of all, it can reduce the flavour.

How to Water Well

Light sprinkling of the surface is a waste of time. Point the spout of the watering can as close to the base of the plant as you can, but make sure you water the soil, not the plant itself. Use a watering can with a fine rose for seeds and seedlings, as very young plants can be damaged or destroyed by heavy droplets of water.

Top Tip

Watering well but occasionally can in many cases accomplish as much if not more than more frequent light watering.

Water Works

You will need to consider the type of soil (*see* pages 5–52) on your allotment when you come to watering, as this will affect how and when you irrigate. Fruit, vegetables and flowers grown in lighter, sandy soils will need watering more often than the same plants grown in a heavier, clay soil, which retains moisture much better.

Fruits

An important time to water plants grown for their fruit, such as tomatoes, cucumbers, marrows and peas, should be when the fruits are beginning to swell or the plants are starting to flower. This is when energies are focused on fruiting and flowering and root growth is restricted. These plants tend to need watering regularly, so keep testing the soil.

Roots

Watering root crops should be targeted at making what's underneath the soil flourish and not the foliage, so try to prevent the soil from drying out. Crops such as onion, swede, beetroot and turnip are less thirsty than other vegetables and once they have been watered in and have established, they can do without watering except in really hot summer.

Finger Test

Soil can be deceptive; it may appear moist but be bone dry underneath. A good way of deciding whether your plants need watering is to stick one of your fingers into the soil. A healthy soil will have moisture down to about 12 cm (4$\frac{1}{2}$ in) to encourage healthy roots.

Save Water

Water is often in short supply in summer, so it makes sense to conserve what moisture there is in the soil and to take measures to lessen the need for watering. In hot weather get into the habit of doing less cultivation, pulling up weeds by hand and hoeing very shallowly. Evaporation is increased every time fresh, moist soil is exposed to the surface.

Cutting Down

You can also cut down on your watering by:

 Improving the soil structure: Work in as much organic matter as possible.

 Keeping the soil mulched: This will cut down evaporation from soil in summer.

 Cultivating across on a sloping allotment: This minimizes water run-off down the slope.

 Remembering to weed continually: Weeds compete for water.

 Building windbreaks around vegetables: These cut down evaporation caused by wind.

 Collecting rainwater in a butt: This will ensure a ready supply of rainwater close to hand.

Good Sense of Humus

Plants guzzle water from the soil so it helps to make it as moisture retentive as possible. Humus (see page 88) is the ideal material as it absorbs many times its own weight in water, so helping to replenish levels by digging in compost or composted manure will help conserve water in the soil. This will be such a boon if your soil is light, lacking in organic matter and too easily draining.

Weeding

Question: When do I need to weed? Answer: All of the time. Sad but true, no matter what technique you use, be it forking over the ground in spring, cutting weeds down as soon as they flower or spraying them with chemicals, weeding is as perennial as some of those thugs muscling on to your allotment.

Why Weed?

Weeds are more than ugly intruders. They are direct competitors for everything your fruits and vegetables hold dear: food, water and light. They host pests and can all but smother your seedlings, so it pays to get rid of them, and get rid of them quickly.

How Often?

How often you weed will depend on how weed infested your allotment is and the type of weeds (see pages 178–84). Regular weeding in short bursts is perhaps the least demoralizing way to attack the problem. Timetabling 15 or 20 minutes of each allotment visit to weeding should make the task less daunting. It is also a good idea to weed as you plant to avoid having to devote entire days or even weeks to the thankless task.

How?

Conventional wisdom for blitzing weeds was through using chemicals such as glyphosate, which are absorbed into the plant they touch but break down as soon as they hit the soil. According to the manufacturers, glyphosate is harmless to people, other animals and the environment. An organic option, other than the hand and fork, is mulch (see page 107).

Head for Cover

Mulch is especially popular on an allotment, not only because chemicals may annoy more organically minded neighbours, but because hoeing can damage crop roots and dry out the earth. Polythene is a commonly used mulch because it is light and easy to handle. It totally blocks out light so seedlings of annual weeds cannot develop while perennial weeds, at the very least, are held in check.

Did You Know?

Using dark polythene has a cooling effect on the soil and is a good weed suppressant for summer; but it prevents air and water reaching the soil and can take a couple of years to kill weeds.

Blanket Coverage

Mulch is also popular on the allotment because it allows you to maximize space on your already flourishing plot: as well as blocking out weeds, it lets you grow your vegetables through the cover. There are two ways of doing this with polythene and other synthetic mulches. Plant your crop first, make cross-like slits in the polythene where the vegetables will poke through and then ease the sheeting over the plants and on to the ground.

Alternatively...

Lay the polythene on the ground, cut small cross-slits in the sheeting where the vegetables are going to emerge through the soil and plant through the slits into the soil. Whichever method you use, the sides and ends of the mulch need to be buried in the soil or weighted down with bricks.

Five of the Worst

Before treating your weeds, you will need to find out what they are:

- **Japanese knotweed:** One of the most invasive weeds, this monster can strike fear into more than the allotment gardener. The UK Government has produced guidance on its treatment, so if found on your plot, have a word with the local authority or the allotment association leader.
- **Bindweed:** This deep-rooted perennial with white or pink flowers can be dug out if you are willing to burrow up to 5 m (16½ ft) to root out the entire network. Alternatively, try weedkiller or the slow-burn approach of mulching the affected area, but this could take months.
- **Nettle:** This persistent creeping pest likes humus-rich soil and spreads through the twin attack of rhizomes and seeds. They should be dug up and the ground forked over. Pluck out anything that looks like a piece of root – it will only come back to haunt you.
- **Dandelion:** Dig out this pretty perennial by hand with a small trowel. Each one of the seeds on a dandelion clock – so irresistible to blow – can grow into a tap-rooted monster if it lands on your soil. Heavily infested areas may have to be mulched.
- **Chickweed:** This annual weed is fairly easy to blitz as long as you do not let it seed. Act fast, though, this little pest can colonize beds and smother seedlings.

When is a Weed Not a Weed?

A weed can be any plant growing in the wrong place and not just perennials such as ground elder. Out-of-control potatoes that have resprouted themselves in the flowerbed or fruit area will also need to be tamed.

Chemistry Lesson

If chemical control of weeds is your preferred option, then take care. The slightest mishap can send a fine chemical mist over your prized marrows and rule out any rosettes that year. Remember to wear overalls, gloves and a facemask.

Read the Packet

Make sure that you read the instructions for recommended use from the supplier. They should give you an idea of the quantities to spray and how far from the plant you should stand when applying the product.

Pesticides

It may be the weeds poking through your allotment path that does it, or perhaps the slugs eating your cabbage leaves will prompt you to think about using a spray called a pesticide. The term 'pesticide' covers a wide range of products, including:

- **Weedkillers**
- **Slug pellets**
- **Fungicide sprays**
- **Animal repellents**
- **Insecticides**

Using a Pesticide

The label on the pesticide bottle will explain how to use the product safely. You may need to keep children and pets away from treated areas, or you may need to wait for

a certain length of time before eating the fruit or vegetables you have treated.
Always:

 Read the label before you buy the product.

 Follow the instructions carefully.

 Where necessary, dilute the product with water and apply it evenly.

 Make up no more than you need to use on that day.

 Do not mix a stronger solution than advised.

 Wash your hands when you have finished spraying.

Alternative Methods

Weed control does not have to come from a bottle or a sheet of mulch. It can come from the most unlikely places and sources, for example:

 Spent manure: Cover the ground with a layer of spent manure, which not only stifles weeds but enriches the soil.

 Living mulch: Try growing a low-growing plant such as trefoil around your vegetables, which smothers the weeds.

 Wood chips: Cover the soil between plants with a thick layer of wood chips, which will smother weeds and can be dug into the soil at the end of the season.

Organic Growing

Many plot holders are choosing the organic route to gardening on their allotment. There are several reasons why people are opting for a more natural approach. Some allotment gardeners are shocked at the number of artificial additives going into much of the produce at their local supermarket. News stories on pesticides and the science of genetic modification have flamed fears, and going organic is perhaps their way of having more of a say in what ends up on their tables. This means taking a firmer grip of how to tend and manage your plot.

Eco-allotments

Growing healthy fruit and vegetables and preventing pests and diseases on the allotment are hard enough even with the chemical pesticides and herbicides to hand. Throwing the bottles and packets off the allotment altogether is a brave step and will involve looking at more natural alternatives.

Going Green

An organic allotment is said to be more environment- and people-friendly. To be truly organic the plot holder has to look at every aspect of growing from preparing the soil to harvesting the crop. Organic gardening involves:

- Avoiding using chemical substances on your plot.
- Encouraging beneficial wildlife to live on your allotment.
- Using compost and organic fertilizer to improve your soil.
- Improving plant health by 'companion' planting – twinning two plant types that benefit each other (*see* page 137).

✔ Pulling out weeds by hand and fork instead of spraying them.

Is It or Isn't It?

Opting to go organic may sound simple on the allotment, but what is organic? That manure may appear natural enough, but how was the horse it came from reared and was it a healthy beast or packed full of antibiotics? Likewise, that scrap of carpet that would make an ideal mulch could be awash with synthetic materials.

The good thing about organic gardening is that you tend to save money by foregoing all those expensive non-organic fertilizers, herbicides and pesticides. The bad news with going organic on the allotment is the labour intensity of digging up weeds instead of spraying them, or the time it takes to kill them with mulch.

Top Tip

Organic methods can be hard work, so it may be smart to dedicate a small amount of time to jobs like weeding by hand – do a little a lot of the time.

Natural Forces

Success with weeding without the use of chemicals is easier with annuals like groundsel, which can be pulled up by hand or hoed off when young. Marestail, on the other hand, can be removed only with deep digging to attack that taproot. Chances are you will never totally eradicate perennial weeds, so be prepared to go back and dig from time to time.

Keep Digging

If you have persistently bad weeds and can leave ground out of cultivation for some time, you can turn the soil. By digging the plot and turning each spadeful over you will expose the roots to the light and air and they should dry out and die. Like other forms of weeding, however, expect to pick out stragglers that survived the first cull.

Good Companions

A useful organic pest control for allotment holders is the art of companion planting. The aim of this is to confuse the pests and keep them off your plants. It also chimes with the organic allotment holder's natural affinity with biodiversity by ensuring a wider array of plants are going into the ground. Some people swear by companion planting and its folkloreish charm. Others take it with huge dollops of salt.

Floral Friends

Examples of companion planting include:

- **French marigolds:** Marigolds are said to contain chemicals that repel wireworms in tomatoes, potato cyst nematodes and slugs.
- **Lavender:** This scented beauty is said to be loathed by many pests but is good for attracting beneficial insects such as bees and butterflies.
- **Nasturtiums:** These are said to release a scent that many pests detest, but they can

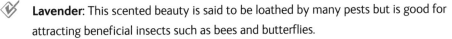

also attract blackfly, so some plot holders use nasturtiums as a decoy to lure the pest away from high-priority crops.

Compromising Circumstances

You may not have the fortitude or the time to quit chemicals outright, but there are ways of giving a few nods in the direction of organic growing. Before you buy or use any pesticide, you could ask yourself whether it is really necessary to control the pest or weed and whether there is an alternative to traditional chemical use.

Instead of reaching for the chemical or pellet, it may be kinder to remove problem weeds with a garden fork or use a physical barrier to keep slugs and snails off your salad leaves.

If You Must...

If you feel you must use a pesticide:

- **Avoid buying more than you will need for one year.**
- **Do not buy products on the internet until you have checked they are legal to use in the UK.**
- **Use it very sparingly and ensure none of it drifts in the wind.**

Always Ask

Other ways of being more environmentally conscious when using chemicals is to never pour them down the drain, a loo or sink because this could harm wildlife and contaminate water. Ask your local authority for advice on disposing of unwanted pesticides or empty containers.

Allotment Gardening if You're Short On Time

Considered opinion has it that the more time you spend on the allotment, the more you will achieve. For this reason many would-be allotment holders never step foot on a plot, fearing backbreaking workloads that will eat into their precious time away from the workplace. However, high-speed gardening on the allotment is becoming more widespread as an increasingly diverse range of people flock to their local sites all over Britain and Europe. Many of these people are in their working prime and want to combine busy careers with active and productive interests.

Quickly Does It

At first sight, this kind of rapid-response growing of fruit and vegetables seems to go against the spirit of the allotment, a place redolent of relaxation and a slower pace of life. In fact, it reflects some of the finest principles that should be applied if an allotment is to prove productive.

Your aim is to streamline workload on the plot so that you can hit a harmonious balance between time spent on and off the allotment; for some people this is every weekend and a few evenings a week, for others it means half an hour every day.

No Time Wasters

All too often, allotment gardeners arrive with good intentions only to 'faff' around for half an hour on tinkering little jobs or to spend a whole day on such a backbreaking task they lose heart and give the plot a miss for the next two weeks. One of the most important principles is to do the right thing at the optimum time, which means working with – rather than against – the soil and the weather.

Make It Easy For Yourself

You can make life on the allotment easier if you:

 Use narrow plots with paths in between so you can step over beds.
 Apply mulch around plants to save you having to water.
 Use salvaged pavers on paths to keep out the weeds.
 Choose plants that are not too tricky or time consuming to nurture.

The 'No-dig' System

Digging takes time and effort and can also damage soil structure. So once you have weeds under control, good drainage and balanced nutrients in the soil, why not give it a miss and give the no-dig system a go? Keeping your beds covered by organic matter to avoid disturbance and compaction enables you to sow seeds into the top layer. Worms drag down the organic matter to aerate the soil and improve its structure. They, in effect, are your diggers, and this saves time.

Raised Beds

Another time- and labour-saving trick on the plot is to make raised beds enclosed in surrounds made of old planks, sawn logs or bricks. These are filled with carefully worked fertile soil and organic matter, which is kept in place by the wooden planks. Raised beds have many advantages. The soil is loose and crumbly so, again, no digging. They warm up quickly, are good for drainage and all you need to do is add a little organic matter from time to time and fork it through.

Quick Choice

Choosing which plants to grow on an allotment where time is everything is a fine art. A knee-jerk response is to go for the crops solely for their ease of growing and nothing else, but row upon row of onions and root crops could lead to overproduction, waste and sheer boredom. Plan your needs in advance and add into the mix a few unusual treats that taste best fresh from the soil or are expensive to buy such as artichoke and asparagus. You can also consider buying plants instead of seeds, especially for more exotic fare like aubergines and peppers.

Giving Yourself a Head Start

Buying small or plug plants (see page 96) has many time-saving godsends:

- ☑ **The companies that grow them are experts and take out all the fiddly jobs such as pricking out.**
- ☑ **By growing the plants in controlled conditions, they take out the risk of frost.**

Short but Sweet

The plants-versus-seed argument strikes at the heart of this kind of plot holding: while more seasoned hands frown at using anything other than seed on an allotment, the pressed-for-time alternative will think of anything to save time, even if it means spending a bit more money.

Keeping Up Appearances

However, carving out the time-consuming fat of working on an allotment does not mean you are dropping your guard. The short but regular bursts of activity that characterize the workload of time-saving allotment holders have one great advantage: plot holders get to see their beloved patch every day. This enables them to develop an intimate knowledge of what makes it tick, when it needs watering and when it needs weeding. Unlike the absentee allotment holder who has to rely on neighbouring growers to keep an eye on the patch for their long stretches away, you are right at the coalface, spearheading productivity.

More Time-saving Tips

Other ways to trim time wasting:

- ☑ **Watch out for crops that are susceptible to pests such as brassicas and try others that can be left for longer periods without attention.**
- ☑ **Perennial fruit bushes are always a good low-maintenance – and therefore time–saving – option as they need less care than annual fruits.**
- ☑ **Plant more perennial ornamental flowers, which will keep weeds down.**

Checklist

 Planting seed on your allotment is the easiest way of sowing: All you do is plant it outside and directly into the soil.

 Before sowing, you need to prepare the beds: Clear the soil of weeds and stones and rake it into a fine tilth.

 Cloches and mini polytunnels protect your plants: They raise soil and air temperature to extend the growing season and the range of crops.

 When you start transplanting seedlings, work quickly and efficiently: Seedlings are fragile and their stems and rootballs should be treated carefully.

 You may need to spend around 15 hours a week on the plot: Jobs include sowing and planting, weeding and watering.

 Weeds are bad in several ways: They compete with crops for soil nutrients, water and light, and they can host pests.

 An organic allotment can save you money: It rules out having to buy expensive non-organic chemicals, but it is more time consuming and harder work.

Harvesting Fruit and Vegetables

When to Harvest

Harvesting your produce is an important date in the allotment calendar. It is the day for you to pick, or harvest, your fruit, vegetables and flowers. It can also be one of the most rewarding tasks on the plot. This is when all your toil, all that weeding and watering, all those long, wet spring days digging and sowing with frozen fingers suddenly seem worth the effort. The moment your allotment reaches the point of bursting ripeness signals the end of many months of hard work. Almost.

It's Not Over 'Til It's Over

Harvesting is a lot more than sneaking the occasional strawberry or popping a pea into your mouth. Shifting buckets of soft fruit or barrows of root vegetables can be a tough task, and it can be far from the sun-baked pastoral images you had in mind of a gentle midsummer harvest, trug in hand.

Don't Delay

Don't shirk the job or put it off, however overcast those skies. Harvesting should always be a number one priority, for the whole point of tending an allotment is to create fresh produce – and the fresher the better. Leave it for too long because the thought of skirmishing with those prickly fruit bushes today is too much and you could throw away some of the year's hard work.

In the Summertime

In fact, though summer is when things start to take off, while you whip off all those fruits and vegetables, most allotments are productive throughout the year. Some vegetables can be picked within a few weeks of sowing, so a good harvester is an alert harvester, lying in wait to pluck fare at its finest.

Never a Dull Moment

Efficient harvesters find themselves collecting bounty throughout the year because they have thought ahead at the earliest stage of the crop cycle on what they want to eat throughout the year. They then plant accordingly to ensure enough winter leeks and spring beans. This is a great way of ensuring you don't have too much backbreaking toil all at once in the heat of summer. Spreading your crop over the seasons may also focus your mind on what you want and when you want it, and this could help you avoid a glut.

Glutton For Punishment

The words 'glut' and 'harvest' go well together and stories of courgette production gone berserk are legendary. Some people have even written books dedicated to harvest gluts, yet right now is a wonderful chance to share in your productivity – or over-productivity. It is also a time to tease friends and family to your table and show them just what they could achieve if they were to take on an allotment.

Last Harvest

Harvesting is a job best left to the end of a plot visit because by saving the picking of fruit and vegetables to the last gasp, you ensure their freshness. Even a couple of hours stretched out in the sun are enough to make your finest harvested produce wilt and lose some of its freshness.

Bringing In the Harvest

Harvesting can be fairly easily built into your busy allotment schedule:

- **In the winter months:** At the start of the year you can balance harvesting Brussels sprouts, celery, winter cabbages, kale and leeks with other jobs on the plot such as sowing summer cauliflowers, cutting down autumn-fruiting raspberry canes and digging over the soil to prepare for sowing.

- **In the spring months:** From April onwards you can start thinking of picking your broccoli, asparagus, broad beans and radishes on a typical visit, which could round off a day hoeing weeds, planting out globe artichokes and sowing beetroot and carrots.

Top Tip

Whenever possible, harvest crops and eat them as soon as you can to get them at their best and freshest.

In the summer months: Brace yourself for bumper harvests of French beans, runner beans, marrows and courgettes, peas, potatoes and strawberries, raspberries and currants. But you can also be getting on with staking runner beans and planning what you want to plant next year.

Long, Hot Summer

Do not expect the job of harvesting to be a quick once over with a fork and secateurs. Picking your produce can take time and even take an entire visit to the plot in more bountiful seasons. But however tricky or time consuming it appears, try to avoid leaving ripe produce in the ground or on plants.

Little but Often

Though the end of your visit is an optimum time to gather produce, it is a good idea when you first arrive on the allotment to make a quick mental note of what you need in your larder that night or week. This again focuses the mind on what allotment gardening is all about – putting fresh food on the table. It will also help you hone your planting plan in future seasons to guard against those dreaded mountains of courgettes. A good rule of thumb on the allotment is to harvest little but often.

Keep the Good Times Coming

Even if your trug is full, you may still want more produce as the summer edges towards autumn, so to keep vegetables cropping longer you could:

 Water plants regularly in hot weather to prolong crops, and harvest often.

 Protect plants like tomatoes and aubergines from cooler temperatures.

How to Harvest

Harvesting is a fine art and it will pay to lavish as much time and attention on perfecting that art as other aspects of allotment gardening such as sowing. How you harvest each crop can have a big impact on several factors: its taste, how well it will store and whether you can expect a second harvest from the same plant. In fact, how you harvest is as important as the harvest itself. Imagine how those prized French marigolds would look in your trug with jagged stems and dog-eared petals, all the result of sloppy harvesting.

Harvesting In Heat

Most allotment holders who come to harvesting in summer face a similar quandary. How can they keep their fruit and vegetables as crisp and fresh as possible in the heat? Salad crops, for example, with their high water content, can start to flop almost as soon as you have harvested them.

Make an Early Start

To avoid salad crops wilting, pick these early in the morning before the sun takes its toll. Watering them an hour prior to harvesting will give enough time for your lettuce and cucumber to absorb the water, but try to avoid watering tomatoes immediately before picking as this can reduce the intensity of their flavour.

Cold Storage

If you are harvesting on a hot summer's day it might be worth investing in a cool box to pop your most sun-sensitive fruit and vegetables out of the heat. Some allotment holders even bring to the site bags of ice – anything to prolong the freshness of their produce. If you made a mental check of what you wanted to pick on your last visit you can hone your harvesting to a tee by bringing exactly the right amount of storage.

Tools of the Trade

Harvesting, like other allotment jobs, is made easier with the right tools, including:

- **Small sharp knife**: A simple kitchen knife with a serrated edge and a sturdy grip will enable you to cut your way through the tough stems of marrows and artichokes.
- **Secateurs**: These are useful for snipping flowers, but you can also use a good pair of kitchen scissors to trim delicate produce like herbs.
- **Hand-held digging fork**: This is an essential harvesting tool and can be used for gently easing root vegetables out of the ground.
- **Containers**: Stock up on boxes, baskets, bags and plastic tubs. Put your salad leaves in the bags, soft fruit in tubs and your root vegetables in cardboard boxes.
- **Gloves**: You may want to wear gloves while you are tugging at those roots and snipping those prickly gooseberry bushes.

Regular Harvesting

Regular harvesting is always a sound objective as it generally makes plants more productive and healthy. But like all things, there's a right way and a wrong way to do it. The important thing is to make the right cut. Herbs with crowns, for example, such as parsley and rocket, need to be taken back to the base of the stem using scissors or a small knife. Herbs with leaves along the stem such as mint should be snipped where leaf meets stem.

Wield the Knife

Having brought all the tools on to the plot, try to use them rather than take short cuts. Why twist plants off their stems, for example, when a neat cut from a blade is so much tidier and less strenuous? Take your knife to a courgette, slice where the fruit joins the plant and you can almost assure yourself an easy cut and a tidy looking plant that is less likely to die back.

Root Crops

Root crops are fairly easy to harvest, but few allotment holders realize that sprinkling water on to a hard and crusty surface in summer can make lifting the crop that much easier. A well-placed trowel or fork will smooth out the job as you pull the crown gently with your other hand.

Peas and Beans

Speed is the essence, because time is always against the pea and bean picker. It pays to leave this harvesting job to the very last and pod the peas as soon as you get home – within an hour or two of picking your produce the sugar turns to starch and the sweetness is lost for ever. Start at the bottom of the plant and work up.

Soft Fruit

Harvesting soft fruit can be a daunting task when you look at all the berries on all the bushes. The trick is to harvest small sections of a large bush at a time or approach a small bush in one go. This might be a good time to cut away any unruly branches or stems.

Picking

Plucking berries or currants is a simple but delicate task, so try to take care. Throw carefully picked but soft raspberries into a container any old how and the resulting mush will ruin your day. Having harvested your fruit, lay it down carefully in the right container. Raspberries, strawberries and blackberries should be layered carefully in their plastic tubs so none is crushed by the weight of others. These containers go on top of all the boxes holding root vegetables after the day's harvest.

Storing Your Harvest

Once you have gathered all your harvested produce you will be surprised by the number of ways you can keep it. Storing, freezing, drying and canning will help you prolong your harvest and enjoy the produce throughout winter and beyond.

Find the Bolthole

The best place to store produce is somewhere dry, airy and cool; away from damp and the frost. Your allotment shed will probably not do, but a garage could be just the bolthole. Storing produce at home is also beneficial because it means you can look – and smell – for early signs of rot.

Where to Put it All

Where and how you store food depends on the fruit or the vegetable:

- **Potatoes:** Keep them in a dark, well-ventilated space to stop them sprouting, and put them in paper or cloth bags, which will not trap condensation.
- **Onions:** Ideally onions, shallots and garlic, as well as squash and pumpkins, can be strung up in a cool, dry place to allow air to circulate around the skins; in theory shelves should be avoided as they prevent air movement around the entire skin.
- **Apples:** Picked on a dry day, apples should be wrapped in greaseproof paper and boxed in a cool, dry place.
- **Beetroot:** Along with carrots, celeriac and swede, beetroot should be stored unwashed in crates, sandwiched between layers of sand or sawdust.

One Bad Apple

The old adage about 'all it takes is one rotten apple' is all too true on the allotment. Any fruit or vegetable showing the smallest sign of decay should go straight on the compost heap. That one bad apple or potato left in storage will ruin the entire crop.

Leave It In the Ground

Some vegetables – carrots, Jerusalem artichokes and leeks – are very easy to store. Just leave them in the ground and harvest when you need them – but relying on this kind of storage could serve up your leeks for slugs to enjoy before you do, and if your soil is prone to waterlogging it may be better to pull them up.

Storing Your Seeds

Saving and storing seeds from your plants after harvest is easily done in late summer and early autumn when many plants like herbs have produced seed heads. Choose a sunny day so the seeds are as dry as possible and cut off the whole seed head – avoid snapping it off as this will shake off many of the seeds. Tap the seeds into a brown paper bag and put them in separate boxes, remembering to mark them. Seeds in berries should be collected when the fruit has just gone overripe.

Canning or Bottling

It must have been a bumper year if you have reached this page and are toying with what to do with all that surplus produce. All that processed food, all those additives are quite enough to frighten many allotment holders, but unpopping a sealed container in the dead of winter is a delicious way of enjoying healthy produce canned straight from the allotment.

The Process

Canning and bottling are simple processes, and the key item is the jar. This is a glass container with a lid and band, which forms an airtight seal when closed. The main reason for canning is to exclude air and completely seal the bottles by vacuum to lock in as much taste and texture as possible. It also ensures all bacteria on the fruit and in the bottle is eliminated. Acidic fruits are often the best to bottle as the acid in the produce helps to maintain sterilization. Vegetables do not normally contain a lot of acid, and so a solution of lemon, salt and water can be used.

Top Tip

When canning fruit or vegetables, never use jars with chipped rims or lids, which could compromise the airtight seal.

Fruit Canning

Canning is a simple process but a few principles apply:

- Use fruit that is unblemished and not too ripe, and grade it to keep the fruit in each bottle about the same size.
- Pack the fruit firmly – without crushing - into sterilized jars that are rinsed and wet inside and fill them to within 2 cm (¾ in) of the top.
- Fill the jars with water or syrup made from one part sugar to four parts warm water.
- Seal the lids securely and sterilize by standing the jars in a saucepan with enough boiling water to cover them completely. Boil for up to 20 minutes.

Storing Your Jars

When you have finished canning and the jars have cooled, remember to label the container with the name of the produce and the date of harvesting. Store the jars in a cool, dark place and eat within a year. Always check the produce and seals before opening a new jar and treat with suspicion any fruit or seal that seems to have deteriorated.

Seal of Approval

You can test the seal after 24 hours by removing the lid clips and lifting the bottles carefully by the lids: if they remain tight and secure, the seal is good. A good size of jar for allotment canners is 500 g (1 lb 2 oz) or 1 kg (2 lb 4 oz).

Drying

Drying food is the oldest form of food preservation, which for centuries was carried out just using salt and sunlight. Drying is a good way of preserving your harvested produce for many months and intensifying its taste. The process of evaporation boosts flavours, and tomatoes and peppers have always been popular in their wrinkly dried state. Though Britain and northern Europe cannot compete with Spain or Italy on climate, allotment holders in every corner of Europe can still dry their produce.

Drying-off Period

If you don't have the climate but do have a greenhouse on your allotment or a conservatory at home, you can lay fruit and vegetables on a tray under the glass for three or four sunny days. You will know when your food is dry by its leathery feel and crinkly state, which is totally free of moisture.

How to Dry

Drying like this is done on trays or from net sacks strung up from the ceiling, but there are other ways of drying, including:

 Oven drying: Slice the vegetable into sections, remove the seeds and place it on a baking tray on a low heat overnight with the door left ajar to allow the moisture to escape.

 Electric dehydrating: This machine has shelves for the vegetables, a heat-control system and a fan to maintain air circulation during the drying process.

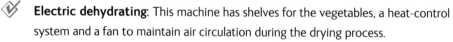

Dry Run

Drying is suitable for tomatoes, chillies and peppers and fruit such as apples and apricots. In their dried state they should be tough but crisp, and when you have sapped all the moisture from your produce tear off a corner. If you can see any traces of juice along the tear, it is not dry enough. The key is to keep temperatures neither too high nor too low – too cool could encourage bacteria, too hot will cook the food instead of drying it, reducing its flavour and nutritional goodness.

Drying Times

Vegetables should be dried in single layers on trays, and drying times vary:

- Carrots, peeled and sliced, take between six and 12 hours.
- Cauliflower, cut into small pieces, takes six to 14 hours.
- Onions, sliced 1 cm (½ in) thick, take six to 12 hours.

Dry Store

When it comes to storing dried fruit and vegetables, make sure that no moisture enters the container. Dried food absorbs moisture from the air, so ensure that your container is airtight by using a sealable jar or plastic box with a lid.

Top Tip

Herbs for drying should be picked just before flowering on a dry day, tied in bunches and hung up in an airy, dry place: once dry, the leaves can be crumbled and stored in jars.

Freezing

Freezing is one of the most popular ways of preserving food from the allotment and can keep your fruit and vegetables tasting good for several months, but it takes more skill than putting a plastic lunchbox full of raspberries into an over-stuffed freezer and then forgetting about it for a couple of years. If you are to make the most of your frozen food, you have to be as methodical in the kitchen as you were on the allotment.

How Long?

Freezing does not preserve food indefinitely, but the frozen fruit and vegetables from your plot should keep for up to six months. Some deterioration in taste is likely but, with correct care, you can keep this to a minimum.

Freezing By Numbers

Golden rules for freezing fruit and vegetables include:

- Only freeze small quantities at any one time to minimize damage to the structure of the food.
- Divide the produce to be frozen into usable amounts, which will encourage you to whip out the whole container.
- Wrap the fruit and vegetables carefully in cloth or kitchen paper as the intense cold of the freezer can dry out food.
- Always label the food container to help you keep an eye on your own 'sell-by' dates and to help you choose which produce you want.
- Store food in plastic boxes with tight-fitting lids, which are better at protecting your fruit from 'freezer burn'.

Blanching

Some people are happy to wash fruit, let it dry and pack it carefully into the freezer, but others prefer to blanch the fruit or vegetables before putting them into cold storage. This process aims to help the produce retain its flavour and texture during freezing. Vegetables or fruit are plunged into boiling water for about 30 seconds and then dropped into iced water or placed under cold running water. Apples, plums and rhubarb fare well with this method.

Keeping Apart

After blanching, lay the fruit or vegetable on a baking tray or greaseproof paper, spaced apart, and pop into the freezer for a few hours. When they are hard, roll them into a freezer-proof tub and return to the freezer. This technique keeps the fruit from sticking together in clumps and is good for raspberries, redcurrants and blackcurrants.

Top Tip

Some produce should not be frozen such as chicory, cucumbers, endive, kale, radishes and Jerusalem artichokes.

Freezing Vegetables and Fruit

Not all food has to be blanched. Blueberries, for example, freeze well and can keep in the freezer for many months. Asparagus, however, should be washed and trimmed of woody parts, cut in half and blanched for around 3 minutes before being cooled under cold running water. It can then be packed into freezer bags for efficient storage.

In from the Cold

Having frozen your food, you can return it to its former glory by thawing at room temperature. If faster defrosting is needed, submerge the watertight plastic tub in cool or lukewarm water or put it in the microwave, following the microwave instructions. Serving it as soon as the fruit defrosts will bring back all the joys of your summer harvest. All vegetables can be cooked from their frozen state except corn-on-the-cob, which should be partially defrosted. Cook frozen vegetables in a small amount of water, but only until tender.

Checklist

☑ **Harvesting is one of the most important jobs in the allotment calendar:**
It is also one of the most rewarding, when you come to pick the fruits of all
your hard work.

☑ **Most plot harvesters find themselves collecting bounty throughout
the year:** They have planned what they want to eat and planted accordingly.

☑ **If you are harvesting on a hot summer's day, it might be worth investing
in a cool box:** You can pop your most sun-sensitive fruit and vegetables out
of the heat to keep them fresh.

☑ **The best place to store
produce is somewhere dry,
airy and cool:** This will keep
your fruit and vegetables free
from damp and away from
the frost.

☑ **You can bottle your produce
in sealed containers:** This is
a delicious way of enjoying
healthy produce canned
straight from the allotment.

☑ **Drying fruit and vegetables
can intensify their taste:**
Do this at home on trays or
in net sacks strung from
the ceiling.

Troubleshooting

Pests

Pests come in all shapes and sizes but have one thing in common: they are all pests, be they small and sometimes deadly aphids or slugs, or the larger four-legged fiends such as cats and rabbits. They are cunning, but you are more so. Armed with the knowledge of which pests attack which plants can help you fight your foes with vigour. With pests – much like diseases and weeds – the message is clear: anticipate, be prepared and take precautions. The maxim about prevention being better than cure has never been so apt than on the allotment.

Check and Check Again

One of the best forms of prevention is to check plants at their most vulnerable stage. Early spring is a great time to get on to the allotment and undertake a thorough pest patrol. This is when young plants are most at risk, so peel back leaves, rummage around the root vegetables and wade into that fruit bush. Some people want a pristine allotment and will spray for every possible pest, and there are those who resign themselves to never eradicating all the slugs and settle for controlling the problem.

A Balanced Approach

Most allotment holders rely on a mixed approach to control: peeling off caterpillars from leaves and stamping on snails, using cultural techniques such as crop rotation to reduce the problem, and resorting to chemicals if things get out of hand.

Steps You Can Take

There are several ways to reduce the problems caused by pests:

- **Rotate your crops**: By growing different types of crops in the soil from season to season you reduce the chance of soil-borne pests taking a hold. Potatoes grown in the same piece of allotment year on year, for example, may suffer from a build-up of eelworm in the soil.

- **Start with strong healthy crops and grow them well**: Try to buy seeds and plants from reputable sources, even if this means spending a little more. You can also check that the variety you want to grow has disease resistance. Keep an eye on new and better varieties.

- **Create an environment that discourages pests**: Cloches, for example, keep out slugs as well as birds and flying insects, while nets or horticultural fleece also offer protection, but ensure that protection – whatever you choose – goes up before the pest has established itself.

- **Remove the problem beast as soon as it arrives**: This is where regular rounds on your allotment pay off well. As soon as you see your lettuces reduced to a few jagged leaves, you know it is time to grab the slug pellets or put up barriers to keep them off your produce.

Did You Know?

You can buy pheromone traps, which use a synthetic hormone to attract and trap various plant pests such as moths.

Worst of the Worst

Everyone has problems with pests on their allotment, so it helps to know your enemy, where you are likely to find it and how you can combat it.

Aphid

There are hundreds of different types of aphids, including greenflies and blackflies, which attack most plants on the allotment, including beans, cabbage and lettuce. They breed like crazy, spreading viruses as they move from plant to plant. Telltale signs include a honeydew secretion on leaves, which leads to a sooty-mould fungus.

 Treatment: Encourage ladybirds, hoverflies and lacewings; choose resistant varieties; plant beans early under cover; use horticultural fleece; wash off with soft soap or insecticide soap.

Cabbage Root Fly

This fly attacks all kinds of brassicas, including cauliflowers, Brussels sprouts and broccoli, by boring into the plant and overwintering in the soil. Damage can be absolute, causing the plant to wilt and collapse.

 Treatment: Put collars, small discs of carpet, around the plants at ground level and cover them with fleece. Dig over the ground in winter to expose the maggots and draw the birds.

Cabbage White Caterpillar

Yellow and black with hairs all over, the cabbage white caterpillar can destroy young plants if left undetected and untreated. They are found on outer leaves of brassicas and the larvae, which eat cabbage hearts, are green and velvety.

 Treatment: Peel off by hand and prevent them from burrowing into the plant.

Carrot Fly

The tiny flies are easy to miss but the damage caused to carrots, celery and parsnips is not. It is the grubs that do the damage, gobbling roots, causing tops to wilt and leaving red-brown lines on the vegetable, which eventually rots.

 Treatment: Carrot fly is attracted to the smell of carrots, so intersperse rows of the vegetable with onions to confuse the pest. It cannot fly higher than about 70 cm (28 in) off the ground, so surrounding the crop with a low barrier of fleece may keep them out.

Asparagus Beetle

These attractive black and yellow chequered beetles cause ugly damage. If untreated, they can strip a plant of its foliage, before bedding down in the soil over winter. Look out for them on leaves from late spring to late summer.

 Treatment: Pick them off by hand or spray with a natural insecticide, cut off affected stems, clear up all the debris and burn it to kill any overwintering beetles that have not made it to the soil yet.

Red Spider Mite

These mites mainly attack crops under glass but outdoor plants such as cucumber and strawberry are also targets. Almost invisible, the creatures colonize leaves, suck sap and cause the foliage to turn brown, curl and die. Mottled, yellowing leaves and fine webs mark its presence.

 Treatment: Mites like dry conditions, so a fine spray of water twice a day will help, and you can use insecticidal soap or insecticide to control.

Slugs

Slugs can devour an entire row of seedlings and eat twice their body weight in foliage – they adore lettuce and cabbage. Warm, moist weather lures them out at night and they shelter and breed under stones, piles of leaves and soft mulch.

Treatment: Encourage frogs (build a pond), hedgehogs and birds; use dry mulches like wood chips; lay out rotting vegetation, which they prefer to fresh produce; use slug traps – cartons filled with beer and sunk into the ground attract slugs, which fall in and drown.

Rabbits and Squirrels

Squirrels can be a problem, nibbling almost every kind of shoot and digging up freshly planted flower bulbs. Rabbits feast on salad crops and brassica leaves and burrow through the ground.

Treatment: Fence out both pests with chicken wire with a mesh size of 2.5 cm (1 in) – maybe smaller for squirrels. The fence should be around 1.2 m (4 ft) high with about 20 cm (8 in) dug under the soil and angled out at about 45 degrees.

Cats and Foxes

The biggest problem from cats is the litter they make of your entire allotment. Foxes dig shallow holes as they look for worms and scratch around looking for more food.

Treatment: A mesh fence should keep them at bay, but it needs to be a sturdy post and beam frame.

Pigeons and Bullfinches

Pigeons make short work of anything from brassicas, chard, peas and lettuce to seeds and rotting compost. When food is short in the depths of winter, that's where you'll find them: on your allotment. Bullfinches tuck into fruit, so watch those gooseberries and pears, if you have trees.

 **Treatment:** Protect crops with cages or netting either draped over the crop or supported on posts. Try making a bird scarer out of old CDs dangling from string: birds are frightened by shiny surfaces swinging in the breeze.

Companion Planting

The more diverse the planting and wildlife you have in the allotment, the easier will be your job of controlling pests. Companion planting (*see page 137*) is one way of encouraging that diversity. The poached egg plant, for example, attracts useful insects, while cabbages and celeriac make good growing companions because their scents mingle and are thought to confuse would-be predatory insects.

Other Benefits

Other benefits of companion planting include:

- Attracting insects to pollinate crops.
- Encouraging insect larvae that eat aphids.
- Adding colour and interest to the plot.

Top Tip

Get to know your friends from foes and the damage they do: holes in leaves suggest slugs, snails and caterpillars; root attack, larvae; curling leaves, aphids.

Diseases

If nets and traps form the arsenal and allies against pests, your war against disease is more subtle and nuanced. Diseases are caused by bacteria, viruses and fungi with telltale signs ranging from cankers or scabs, black spots, wilting and mildew to malformations and patterned leaves. The damage often starts on one plant and, unless you act fast, it can spread like wildfire through your crop. As well as acting fast, you can plant fast to minimize the chances for disease to thrive.

Resist and Control Disease

A methodical approach to fostering disease resistance on the plot includes buying resistant seed varieties or, where possible, stock that is certified as free from viruses. If you collect seed from your own crops, only keep seed from healthy plants and store it carefully. As soon as disease raises its head in the form of mildew or rot, remove the plant, taking care not to shake spores all over the greenhouse or plot. And don't forget to clean or sterilize tools and pots to minimize the chances of cross infection.

Spray Away

Your fight against outbreaks of disease may involve using chemicals and a sprayer. Always follow the manufacturer's instructions, store sprays away from children, wash equipment after use and avoid spraying on windy days, which could cause the liquid to drift.

Fungi

Some of the most effective strategies for keeping disease off your allotment are the easiest. A good, clean allotment with well-looked-after plants is perhaps one of the best antidotes to the mildews and moulds of this world. Fungi attack plants already weakened through lack of light, food or water. Their tired or damaged tissue is just the chink needed by disease to clamp its iron grip on a plant. Its spores, meanwhile, can remain active in soil for years, so illnesses like clubroot (*see* page 175) can come back to haunt you.

Bacteria and Viruses

Bacteria can enter a plant only through an existing wound caused by nibbling pests, careless handling or pruning. The only action to take when bacteria strike is to cut out the infected

stems or branches until you hit healthy tissue, then keep an eye on that plant. If you act fast when fungi or bacteria strike, you can minimize treatment to maybe picking off a few infected leaves. Viruses are incurable and are spread by sap-sucking insects.

Minimize Risks

Simple measures to minimize the risk of disease on your allotment include avoiding over-watering plants and firming compost too heavily, as this combination can lead to damping off disease. Do not overcrowd plants in beds or pots because this can stunt growth and lead to poor air circulation. Remember, plants will rarely succumb to disease or pests if you create a healthy environment on the allotment.

Worst of the Worst

Like pests, almost every allotment holder will at some point have a nasty brush with diseased plants and, like pests, it helps to know your enemy, where you are likely to find it and how you can combat it.

Blight

This fungus likes warm, wet weather and is spread by the wind and rain on to potatoes and tomatoes. Leaves develop brown patches before falling off, and infected potato tubers break out in dark patches and give off a dreadful stink. Tomatoes turn brown and scaly.

Treatment: Cut off all affected leaves to prevent the spread of the fungus spores into the soil and destroy infected tomatoes. Give plants plenty of space to improve air circulation, spray with a copper fungicide, do not compost infected material and try resistant varieties such as the 'Arran' potato or 'Ferline' tomato.

Top Tip

Use organic chemicals as carefully as their synthetic equivalents; and only when you have identified the problem can you target it accurately.

Blossom End Rot

Poor watering can trigger blossom end rot in tomatoes, aubergines and peppers, as the dried out plants find it hard to absorb calcium. Fruit flowers turn brown and leathery.

Treatment: Regular watering when the fruits are forming is the best way of preventing the ailment: if the soil is too arid, nutrients will not be absorbed properly.

Clubroot

This soil-borne nightmare can devastate cabbages, broccoli, Brussels sprouts, kale and turnips and live in the soil for 20 years. The first you will know about it is when the roots become swollen and distorted into elbow-like 'club' shapes. Clubroot thrives in damp, acidic soil and is easily spread by tools and muddy boots.

Treatment: Improve your growing conditions with fertile, well-drained soil, add lime to acid earth, introduce crop rotation, remove and destroy all infected plants and buy resistant varieties.

Damping Off

Damping off can affect all seedlings on the allotment, causing roots and the base of stems to rot and bringing swift death to young plants. The fungus spreads quickly in damp, poorly ventilated conditions and where poor plant hygiene practices have been allowed to persist on the plot.

Treatment: Sow seeds in clean trays and pots using fresh, good-quality compost. Spray with a copper-based fungicide and water seedlings with mains water.

Chocolate Spot

This is another disease that thrives in damp conditions. Round, brown splotches pockmark the stems and leaves of broad beans, which can eventually kill the plant. However, in most cases the fungal disease is not fatal and you can still harvest the crop.

Treatment: Make sure your broad beans grow on rich soil with good drainage, dig up badly damaged plants, clear weeds and rubbish and treat plants with a fungicide.

Onion White Rot

The payload of this rot includes wilting and yellowing leaves. It is the most widespread disease of the *Allium* family. Whiteflies start clustering around the base of the bulb, which becomes covered in a white, fluffy mould, the spores of which can colonize soil for over 10 years.

 Treatment: There is no chemical control for onion white rot and infected crops should be removed and destroyed. Avoid planting anything from the onion family in the earth for several years.

Downy Mildew

Various types of downy mildew can affect onions and brassicas, and all of them thrive in wet, humid weather. Infected brassicas display a yellowy patch on the leaf. Onion leaf tips turn yellow, which then become blotchy and finally sport a furry white fluff, turning purplish-brown.

 Treatment: Keep plants well ventilated, remove and burn infected debris and spray crops with a copper fungicide.

Powdery Mildew

Powdery mildew is less damaging than downy mildew as it stays on the outside of the plant, though the grey powdery growth can cover any part of a number of vegetables and fruit such as marrow, spinach, strawberries and raspberries. The powder can stunt or distort plant growth.

 Treatment: Overdry root systems can hasten an attack of powdery mildew, so keep plants well watered, and adding mulch in spring can prevent water in the soil evaporating.

Botrytis

All it takes is a wet summer to usher this disease, also called grey mould, on to your allotment to attack ornamentals, vegetables and raspberries and strawberries. The fluffy mould sends spore clouds into the air that also latch on to cucumbers and courgettes with cuts or lesions.

Treatment: Remove dead and infected parts of the plant and avoid overcrowding your crops. Clear up rotting leaves and give plants enough space to improve air circulation.

Gooseberry Mildew

This mildew also affects blackcurrants, leaving a powdery grey fungal growth on leaves, stems and fruit. Badly affected shoot tips and leaves die and fall off and, though the fruit is still edible, the growth can be unpleasant to look at. It strikes in late spring.

Treatment: Remove infected branches as soon as you see the fungal growth. This not only removes damaged material, but encourages better air circulation through the plant. A fungicide spray may help control this mildew.

Cane Blight

This common fungal disease in raspberries starts life at ground level, but the first signs are on the leaves, which shrivel on the older canes. Dark cracks will appear near the ground, from where the fungus entered the plant.

Treatment: There is no cure but raspberries catch the disease through cuts, so be careful when you are digging or weeding around the canes.

Weeds

Weeds will never go away, but don't let that stop you trying to expel them. Some are disruptive, rampant colonizers bent on stealing all the nutrition and water from the soil. In return you get to host a gangly, unwanted plant that itself hosts pests and diseases. Your weed problem will probably be your allotment neighbour's problem too. Most annual weeds multiply by seed that knows no plot boundary, while perennials send down roots that stretch deep and far. If you've got it, chances are your neighbour has it too.

Act Now

The best policy with weeds is to strike from the outset, and a pro-active approach to control is good for both your plants and you. Many allotment tenancy agreements compel you to keep your plot as tidy and weed free as possible to ensure the seeds do not proliferate and spread further afield.

The Stale Seedbed

A good way of giving yourself – and your plants – a head start over annual weeds is to make a 'stale seedbed'. Prepare the bed for

planting, leave it and let the inevitable weeds worm their heads above the soil. Hoe off the weeds and then sow your seeds immediately. This should ensure your seeds are up and running before the weeds come back.

Control Measures

You can't hope to totally destroy all the weeds on your plot, but provided you are vigilant and weed regularly and frequently you should be able to keep on top of the problem.

Some Benefits

The less-is-more approach has other benefits. Though rigorously destroying weeds may give your plot a pristine patina, to some people a few weeds can do more good than harm. In their eyes weeds help to hold together the soil structure – they are a sign of the earth's fertility and prevent nutrients from leaching away from the soil.

Top Tip

Only use approved chemical weedkillers: it is illegal to make home-made weedkiller, while your tenancy agreement will probably forbid dangerous or banned chemicals on site.

Perennial Weeds

The most vigorous and invasive weeds are perennial. Most perennials must be dug up or die a slow, painful death from weedkiller. Their remains should not be composted until the plant is well and truly dead.

The Rogues Gallery

Perennial weeds fall into several categories:

- **Surface creepers**: Look out for brambles, ground ivy and creeping buttercup.
- **Underground creepers**: These include bindweed, ground elder and creeping thistle.
- **Taproot weeds**: Get to know your dandelion, cow parsley and docks.
- **Underground rhizomes and tubers**: These include horsetail, oxalis and wild garlic.

Ground Elder

This is one of the most persistent offenders on the allotment, shedding tiny root fragments every time you think you've sifted the soil clean. Thick leafy foliage can smother small plants while the dense root system can sap the soil of nutrients.

- **Treatment**: Dig up the root, or try the slow-burn approach of covering with plastic sheeting for a year or more.

Dock

Docks throw out big fleshy leaves that provide cover for all sorts of pests such as slugs and snails. They take up space, while their deep taproots enjoy all those nutrients in the soil.

- **Treatment**: Dig out when the soil is moist.

Brambles

Brambles spread rapidly underground and above ground. While the roots are snaking themselves under your feet, long, prickly stems are coiling around your water butt and bean poles. Any strand of bramble that touches the earth can put out its own root system, giving the plant a tenacious foothold.

 Treatment: Cut back the brambles with shears, scythes or mattocks and dig out the root system.

Horsetail

Like other perennials, horsetail survives winter by storing nutrients in its roots and this weed is one of the most pernicious. Roots are usually too deep to eradicate, while its spores ensure it keeps cropping up elsewhere.

 Treatment: Deep digging may check the weed, weedkiller will probably be more effective but is no guarantee, and blanketing the area with carpet may weaken it.

Couch Grass

Tufty-looking grass characterizes the look of couch grass, which spreads underground by rhizomes. The white root system is very invasive, forming large networks of stems below the earth and this weed is a big problem on allotments, which can colonize newly dug beds in a short time.

Treatment: Attack the plant at its weakest, in late autumn or winter, by forking and pulling up by hand. If the plot is matted with the grass you can cut out squares and remove the roots.

Creeping Thistle

Like creeping buttercup, creeping thistle has pretty flowers but can grow up to around 1 m (3 ft) high. The tap and lateral roots fight for space and nutrients in the soil and, on a tight plot of land where space is a premium, this plant is one of the most conspicuous intruders.

Treatment: Dig it up as soon as you see it, keep the ground forked over and rip out the young plants as soon as they appear.

Annual Weeds

Annual weeds last for one year, but unless you are quick their legacy will go on and on. They grow, flower, seed and die in their short one-year life, so to beat them you have to kill the weeds before they set seed.

Cleavers

These are the sticky ones kids just love and allotment gardeners just hate. Cleavers are subtle invaders and before you know it they have thrown out strands of stringy foliage, which can scramble over your plants and eventually smother the younger ones.

Treatment: Fortunately, this is fairly easy to blitz by pulling gently or forking out of the ground.

Hairy Bittercress

This relative of watercress can be eaten when young, but after flowering its seed pods explode at the slightest touch to spread rapidly and put out more generations.

Treatment: Be quick and methodical; dig them up by hand or hoe them off before the little white flowers appear.

Annual Meadow Grass

This plant is the guilty suspect on all those grass allotment paths. It has rough, leafy blades, splayed seed heads and, like all annual weeds, needs to be dug out fast.

 Treatment: Pull it out or mulch heavily infested areas.

Groundsel

Groundsel likes heavy soils, throws out yellow flowers and hundreds upon hundreds of seeds, which are almost guaranteed to take root when they hit the soil.

 Treatment: Pull up or hoe groundsel before it sends all that seed in all those directions.

Speedwell

This plant can grow in a variety of situations, but is mostly found in shady areas with dry, sandy or rocky soils. One of the most noticeable characteristics is the cobalt-blue flowers.

 Treatment: Hoe off young seedlings and pull up more established plants. The shallow roots can be removed by forking over the ground.

Keep on Top of Annuals

Neglect annual weeds at your peril. As soon as they have scattered their seed, you've lost the battle. The best way of avoiding the annual onslaught is to weed often but not slavishly. Whip out the hoe or hand fork every time you see an annual weed. Regular hoeing with a sharp tool will gradually reduce the annual headcount to manageable numbers, and planting up empty beds as soon as possible will help you marginalize the weeds even more.

Another View

Weeding is as much a state of mind as an act on the allotment. Quite often even the most common or seemingly persistent weeds, if kept under reasonable control, pose no more threat than being unsightly and slightly in the way. Some of them even have positive points that almost redeem their presence on the plot.

Good Weeds

Tucked away from the main crops, some weeds can be useful. Black medick, for example, attracts butterflies and bees while fat hen is a focus for hoverflies. Chickweed seeds are a treat for birds, while some people feel the same way about dandelion leaves in salad. Clover feeds nitrogen into the soil and nettles can be cooked just like spinach.

Bad Crops

Some crops that you deliberately grew a season or two ago can take on weed-like status as they spread like wildfire because you left a few stragglers last time you harvested. Potatoes are known to resprout anywhere and everywhere, and rampant chicory roots can take on almost invasive proportions.

Top Tip

To make weeding easier, sow seeds in straight rows and mark each row, so you will know for sure anything that comes up between rows must be a weed.

Checklist

- **There are several ways to reduce the problems caused by pests**: You can rotate your crops, start with healthy crops and grow them well.
- **One of the best forms of pest prevention is to check plants at their most vulnerable stage**: Early spring is a great time to get on to the allotment and undertake a thorough pest patrol.
- **Plant diseases are caused by bacteria, viruses and fungi**: Telltale signs range from cankers or scabs, black spots, wilting and mildew to malformations and patterned leaves.

- **Minimizing the risk of disease on your plot is simple**: Avoid over-watering plants and firming compost too heavily, do not overcrowd plants and encourage good ventilation.
- **Be vigilant with weeds**: Weed regularly and frequently to keep on top of the problem.
- **Some weeds can prove useful if they are tucked away from the main crops**: Black medick attracts butterflies and bees, while fat hen is a focus for hoverflies.
- **Make weeding easier by sowing seeds in straight rows**: You will know for sure anything that comes up between rows must be a weed.

Fruit and Flowers

Fruit Trees

Fruit has played a major part in history, myth and legend. Adam and Eve, after all, were cast out of the Garden of Eden for plucking the apple and sadly your allotment landlord may have done likewise to the tree. Some allotments ban trees outright for taking up too much space and shading other plants. However, many sites will allow dwarf fruit trees. Trees need little care, they blossom in spring and they fruit for years.

Choosing Trees

Choosing soft fruit plants is reasonably straightforward, but trees need more thought. Is there enough room? Even dwarf trees put on a fair amount of spread, while a half-standard tree can stand 1 m (3 ft) tall? Fortunately, bush-type trees can be planted in large pots in the corner of your allotment.

All Shapes

Fruit tree production peaks in mid-maturity, say when a tree is 10 years old, and they can take many exotic forms, including:

- **Whip:** The cheapest and smallest tree, a one-year-old single-stem specimen.
- **Standard:** A semi-mature tree with rootball and a stem of about 1.8 m (6 ft).
- **Bushes:** Look like mini trees and have trunks of around 50 cm (20 in).
- **Espalier:** A stem sprouting branches, which are trained along wires against a wall or fence to grow horizontally.
- **Cordon:** Tree stem grown at 45-degree angles – good if you don't want to shade neighbouring plot holders.

Apple

Apple trees are best planted in the dormant season, between November and spring, but should not be planted in frozen soil. Cut back damaged roots, make a hole in the soil twice as big as the rootball and remove any weeds from the earth. Mulch in early spring from the second year onwards and prune the tree to cut out dead branches or to balance the crown to let in light and air.

Harvest: Gently twist the apple on its stem and if it comes away it is ripe. Store only unbruised apples in screwed up paper and make sure they do not touch each other.

Pear

Plant semi-mature pears in winter or spring and dig in container trees in autumn, preferably in a sheltered, sunny spot of the plot. Soak the roots overnight and plant in a hole with compost. Like other trees, you may want to drive a stake into the ground for support and tie it to the tree. Prune in winter to achieve the desired pyramid-type shape.

Harvest: Fruit is ripe when it parts easily from the tree, but under-ripe pears can be removed and left to ripen. Wrap each pear in tissue paper and store in a cool place.

Did You Know?

You should water trees generously in dry weather in the first season and until the tree roots establish themselves.

Plum

Soak the roots overnight, then plant in a hole with soil, compost and fertilizer. Like other trees, plums should be planted to the same depth it grew in the nursery. From the second year onwards, mulch in early spring with compost or feed with blood, fish and bone. Prune to free up the crown.

Harvest: Taste to check the fruit is ripe and pick when it pulls easily from the tree. Store in a cool, dry place.

Peach and Nectarine

Plant the tree in a sheltered suntrap on the allotment, or nurture in a greenhouse in colder northern climates. Cover small trees with horticultural fleece to protect against frosts and prune to remove dead wood, weak or crossing branches. Keep an eye out for peach leaf curl, which blisters leaves, and spray if needed.

Harvest: Harvest when the fruit looks and feels ripe and comes away with a gentle twist. Store at around 20°C (68°F) for a day to bring out the best flavour.

Apricot

Try to plant on a frost-free, sun-catching spot, in a rich, well-draining, slightly alkaline soil. You should mulch with compost and water regularly in hot weather. Prune the trees in spring while still dormant and cover bushes with netting, also in spring, to protect blossom from frost.

Harvest: Lay fruit in single layers in a tissue-lined box and store in a cool, dark place.

Cherry

Sweet or sour cherries should be planted, like other trees, in the dormant winter season. Sweet cherry needs sunlight, but sour is more tolerant of shade. Both, however, like free-draining soil. Prune to avoid silver-leaf disease, but avoid cutting back in winter.

 Harvest: Early to mid-summer for sweet and later for sour cherries. Cut off the fruit with scissors or secateurs and eat immediately.

Fig

Being Mediterranean, figs need a sunny, sheltered spot but can tolerate poor, stony ground. Mix broken bricks and crockery into the soil. Plant the fig in spring and edge it in with four vertically buried paving slabs to restrict root growth. Mulch in autumn and protect with fleece in winter.

 Harvest: Fruit sagging on weakened stems is a sign of ripeness; gather carefully and store in a single layer in a cool place for several weeks.

Quince

You can plant container-grown trees from November to March. Dig a hole, spread out the roots, scatter a handful of slow-release fertilizer and drive in a support stake. Spray with liquid seaweed in spring and mulch around the base. In summer, prune dead wood and last year's growth.

 Harvest: Leave fruit until it has yellowed and is most flavoursome before picking. Lay the fruit in single layers but not next to apples or pears as the strong scent can taint other fruit.

Berries

Growing soft is no soft option. The plants are delicate and the fruit all too easily damaged or ruined, so it is important to get a good start. Try to buy plants from a reliable source, such as a good nursery, and if possible buy stock that comes with a virus-free certificate. Having brought the strawberry plant back to the nursery, avoid planting it where soft fruit has grown before, and buy some netting: birds love soft fruit as much as you do and can eat it faster than you.

Watering Fruit

Even in milder north European climates, most fruit plants suffer from a water shortage in summer. And with all fruit crops, watering will give you bigger fruits in greater profusion. Your plants will also grow that much better and are more likely to give you heavier crops in years to come. Strawberries and cane fruit such as raspberries and blackberries can do with less watering, but bush fruits such as blackcurrants and gooseberries like to binge on water over a longer period.

Mulching Fruit

Mulches can help fruit as well as vegetables, but ought to be laid in spring before the soil has dried out too much. Polythene mulches are particularly helpful for strawberries and the bush fruits, but not for cane fruits. These will only lift the material, which will blow around the allotment.

Strawberry

Strawberries are usually started from rooted runners, which need to be planted in summer in rich, fertile soil that drains well and is given a helping hand from lots of well-rotted manure. Plants should be spaced at about 40 cm (16 in) intervals in rows around 1 m (3 ft) apart. For added protection, plant through a polythene membrane or lay straw under the fruit to deter slugs. Using cloches will keep birds away.

Harvest: Pick the fruit only when it is completely red; choose a dry day and pinch the fruits away leaving green stems intact. Take care to avoid bruising the fruit.

Did You Know?

It is easy to root new strawberry plants in late summer by pulling up a runner in the soil, leaving it attached to its parent plant and securing it in a pot filled with compost: when it is strongly rooted, sever from the parent.

Gooseberry

Gooseberry bushes should be planted in winter, but are not too fussy about soil conditions. However, a moist soil will help keep away powdery mildew (*see* page 176). Gooseberry does not need heavy pruning but, after fruiting, trim back to allow air to circulate.

Harvest: Ripe berries should drop off into your hand without much prompting and they can be refrigerated for a couple of weeks or frozen in a single layer on a tray.

Blueberry

Blueberries need a well-drained acidic soil of around pH 4.5 to 5.5, so if you have a neutral soil, start forking in an ericaceous, or lime-free, compost. Plant in sun or partial shade and prune in winter, taking out a third of the old or damaged wood.

Harvest: Leave the fruit on the tree for three or four days after it has reached its dark colour. When the berries fall easily from the tree, you know it's ripe. Refrigerate the berries or freeze them on trays.

Raspberry

Healthy raspberries should crop for over a decade. Summer- or autumn-fruiting varieties produce fresh canes every year that grow fruit the next year. They flower in late spring and thrive in a sunny spot. Cut back the canes after harvesting, water well in dry weather and cover with nets in first flower for protection.

Harvesting: Pick on a dry day but only pluck the fruit that pulls away easily, and keep picking, as raspberries soon rot after ripening. Firm berries will keep for four days or so left on a single layer on a tray in the refrigerator. If you have a glut, freeze on trays.

Top Tip

For a good, healthy spread of canes, train seven or eight per plant on to support wires and cut the remaining canes with secateurs.

Blackberry

Another cane fruit, blackberries follow the early fruiting raspberries and should be planted in winter in moist, slightly acidic soil. Soak the rootball before planting. A robust post-and-wire frame will offer good support to a maturing plant and the blackberry should be tied back as it grows to keep from becoming an unkempt tangle. Cut down old canes after fruiting and tie the new ones.

 Harvest: They are ripe when they are soft and fully coloured. Pick on a dry day to prevent the fruit from becoming mouldy, then eat or freeze the produce.

How to Prune

Plants, shrubs and trees can survive and thrive without pruning, but a good cut and trim can maximize harvests and stop the plant overgrowing. This is especially important on an allotment, where space is often tight. The main reason for taking secateurs or lopping tools to a plant is to cut out dead wood, infected material or crossing branches.

Pruning Points

Be careful to make the right kind of cut by:

 Always using sharp tools that are strong enough for the job – secateurs won't be enough for a well-established woody branch.

 Cutting above the node – the knob on a branch or stem that leaves grow from – to avoid the stem dying back.

 Making a sloping cut through the stem in the direction you want the new growth to shoot.

Currants

Fruit growing is often sacrificed if space is at a premium on the allotment, but try to squeeze in a few black-, red- or whitecurrants. Blackcurrants, for example, are deemed one of the most nutritious fruits, packed with antioxidants and vitamin C. What a shame to miss out on such a health fest just because space is tight. Currants also make attractive additions to the allotment, bringing striking colour and form. And when you look at the extortionate cost of a tiny punnet of currants from the supermarket, that empty corner of the allotment suddenly becomes ripe with opportunity.

Small Is Beautiful

These days, currant bushes are not the space gobblers they once were. More compact varieties can be planted together about 1 m (3 ft) apart to achieve a cropping hedge that can double as a highly effective windbreak for the allotment. Fruit such as redcurrants can also be grown as slanted cordons, spaced 30 cm (1 ft) apart and used as a border to your plot path or to form a screen.

Blackcurrant

The main difference between black- and red- and whitecurrants, apart from colour, is the way they are pruned. The latter two plants produce fruit from old wood, but blackcurrants fruit from young, one-year-old shoots. It should therefore be pruned in late summer after fruiting. Blackcurrants can live for many years and rise to 1.8 m (6 ft) high, but look out for compact varieties at your nursery or garden centre.

The bushes like open, sunny and sheltered spots on the allotment, and a good depth of soil. This enables them to stretch out their roots when it comes to planting, which is best done around autumn time or winter. It also pays to pile on organic mulch to retain moisture.

Harvest: The fruit is at its ripest about a week after it has turned black and the fruits begin to swell. The best way of harvesting blackcurrants is to cut off stems bearing the fruit and pick the fruit on the ground or on a table inside your allotment shed. Blackcurrants will keep in the refrigerator for about a week.

Pruning Blackcurrants

Pruning blackcurrants is a much more vigorous task than taking secateurs to red- and whitecurrants. Soon after planting in the first year, cut back the plant to about 2.5 cm (1 in) above ground level. Mature bushes should be pruned in late summer, with a third of the old wood trimmed to the ground.

Top Tip

Growing a range of berries along with strawberries and blackberries can give you ample opportunity to cook delicious puddings and jams, or just eat handfuls of the fruit fresh from the plants.

Redcurrants and Whitecurrants

These two currants are among the most attractive soft fruits, with swags of shiny berries drooping from the bushes in high summer. They make fantastic hedges in allotments and their bounty is great for pies, jellies and jams. There's more good news: red- and whitecurrants are fairly easy to grow. The bushes can be a little fiddly to pick but their saving grace for harvesters is their lack of thorns.

Both bushes grow in the same kind of conditions, which are sunny and on most soil types. Generous lashings of bone meal and well-rotted compost will ensure a good start for young fruit bushes. They should be planted in late autumn, when they are dormant, and before spring growth shoots to life.

Harvesting: Avoid picking berries individually, which is too time consuming. Instead, lop off trusses of fruit when the berries are at their fullest and shiniest, but be choosy because not all the fruit ripens at the same time, so two or three trawls across the bush may be needed. The berries can be frozen or enjoyed straight from the bush.

Top Tip

Currants ripen in super-quick time, so, unless you are quick or have the bushes protected in a fruit cage or with a net, the birds may beat you to the berries.

Planting Cuttings

Taking cuttings from red- and whitecurrants in autumn will enable you to grow your own bushes. Cut a mature stem into 20 cm (8 in) lengths above and below a bud and strip any leaves. Put each cutting in a prepared bed a stem's length apart, leaving only the top bud exposed. Water and cover with polythene with slits so the plants can poke through. Remove in spring and keep watering. In summer, water each bush once a week and add mulch if the soil appears to be drying out.

Pruning Redcurrants and Whitecurrants

Prune young plants in late summer or autumn, but instead of taking branches back to the ground, trim them to a third of their original length. After a couple of years, the mature bush should be pruned in autumn, when you cut back shoots from the side also by a third. This should leave you with a light, airy centre and a compact goblet-like shape. Don't forget, a well-pruned bush is less likely to be struck with disease and is more likely to be easier to pick.

Did You Know?

Redcurrants and whitecurrants are fairly easy to train into cordons and fan-like shapes to make the most of the space on your allotment.

Grapes

Once you have mastered growing more common fruit, you can turn your thoughts to the less usual ones like grapes. First brought to Britain by the Romans, grapes have always been considered one of the toughest challenges on the allotment and elsewhere. In fact, with a favourable site and a little encouragement, this fruit can be both reliable and productive. With climate change suggesting warmer weather in years to come, allotment holders across northern Europe should be able to sup from the cup of good fortune, just like their lucky south European counterparts have been doing for centuries.

Getting Started

A tough reputation they may have, but grapevines can grow in most soils as long as the earth is not prone to waterlogging. A warm, sheltered nook on your allotment that catches the sun could be just the spot for your grapes. If that rules out your shady shed wall, you can always train the vines up a pergola or an arch made on the plot or bought for next to nothing from a garden centre or a DIY store.

Planting

The best time to plunge your vine into the allotment soil is just when winter is turning to spring and the plant is still dormant. Dig a hole twice the size as the rootball, add bone meal and well-rotted manure, and plant to the same depth as the plant was in the nursery.

Care of Young Grapes

With the vine bedded into your plot, you should mulch the surrounding ground. The plant should be able to thrive without fertilizer, but keep it stocked up with well-rotted manure and compost. As the grapevine grows, you will need to support it with a post and horizontal wire support, but the plant must be pruned carefully. Young vines should be allowed to fruit only in their third year, when they should be stripped of all but three bunches of grapes, next year four and so on until they have fully matured.

Pruning

In winter, you should trim the vine as soon as the leaves have fallen, and before Christmas. If you wait until spring, the vine is likely to bleed when cut. In summer, your job is to prevent the vine from running riot and wasting energy putting out metres of useless growth, so cut back fairly often to keep it compact and tidy.

Problems

Grapes, like every other plant on the allotment, need careful nurturing. Botrytis and powdery mildew (*see pages 176–77*) are two diseases that can take hold of your vine. Mulch and water in dry spells to thwart the mildew, and remove affected leaves and thin out the plant to improve air circulation to fight against botrytis.

Top Tip

Check out disease-resistant varieties such as 'Seyval' (white) and 'Boskoop Glory' (black).

Flowers

Allotments throw up enormous opportunities for the trail-blazing grower. The subtle use of carefully chosen flowers can send a delightful shock of vibrancy and colour across even the most utilitarian plot. You can dedicate entire beds to floral extravaganzas or intersperse flowers with vegetables in a decorative plot with echoes of kitchen gardens and potager beds. Blending flowers with salad crops, for example, which are harvested regularly when the crops are small, enables you to space plants more closely than would usually be the case. This allows you to squeeze even more out of your allotment.

Take Your Pick

Sunflowers and sweet peas commonly find a warm and welcoming corner on the allotment, but you can grow virtually any flower for the home right there on the plot, including zinnias and cosmos. Easiest to grow are bulbs, which give a dash of colour in spring and autumn, while annuals will keep colour flowing throughout the summer. Choose varieties that are long lasting and don't sag too soon after you have picked them.

Where to Grow Flowers

Flowers are like most vegetables; they like a sunny place on the plot with enough shelter to spare them a buffeting wind and give you the job of staking them for protection. Not to worry if you can't justify a dedicated bed for your blooms, annual flowers can be blended into a vegetable crop and can be planted somewhere new each year.

Eco-friendly Flowers

There is another bonus to growing your own flowers, and its benefits could stretch many miles beyond the allotment. The cut-flower industry is huge but not without controversy. Millions of flowers are flown or shipped into the UK every year in monster-sized refrigerated containers. Critics argue the flowers are treated with an abundance of chemicals and nurtured by staff with poor working conditions and even poorer wages. Growing your own bouquets seems such an easy alternative.

How to Get the Best Blooms

Many flowers are happy to just do their own thing, but you can help by bearing in mind that:

- Flowers like good compost and some, like sunflowers, are really greedy, craving well-rotted manure.
- Beds edged with flowers create eye-catching pools of colour with all the practical benefits of companion planting (*see* page 137) to keep bad pests at bay.

- If you hold back planting hardy annuals on the allotment plot until March, they are more likely to be spared the later frosts.
- Flowers in need of a bit of oomph get just that with potassium-rich fertilizer, which targets the flowers rather than the leaves.

Sunflower

Sunflowers look great on the allotment and can both physically and visually define parts of the plot. They can also be used to screen unsightly elements such as compost bins. An un-reconstituted sunbather, this beauty likes good soil with compost or manure. Sow seeds in pots from March, while from May you should be thinking of putting them into the bed to flower from July to September.

Sweet Pea

Sweet peas are easy to grow and tough enough to enjoy a long, fragrant and colourful season. They like full sun and a hefty spread of well-rotted compost. Seeds should be sown under cover from October and as soon as they have germinated they can go on to the plot, protected with fleece or a cloche. Water well in summer and train the sweet pea on a bamboo wigwam, fence or your shed wall.

Zinnia

Tall, upright and with velvety petals, Zinnia offers an exotic counterpoint to all those turnips and cabbages. Choose a warm spot with good soil and plant out in late spring. The plant, which comes mainly from Mexico, flowers from July to October. Once established, zinnias can tolerate drought, but watch out for powdery mildew (*see* page 176) in wet weather, and think about staking the stems when the wind gets up.

Cosmos

Colourful cosmos makes a great cutting flower and is easy to grow, so it is a good plant for the new allotment holder and a dead cert to keep children occupied for at least four or five minutes. The flower likes light, well-drained soil and is largely trouble free with disease, but when you come to cut cosmos, cut the stems early or late in the day, not in full sun, which can sap all the plant's energy.

Snapdragon

Snapdragon will add a little old-world cottage charm to your allotment, but will also bring valuable benefits. Slugs, snails and rabbits tend to shy away from the flower, so if other blooms on the plot or your prized vegetables are under siege, a nearby snapdragon could be their guardian angel. Bees on the other hand love nothing more than clambering in and out of the petals. Good soil and dappled shade should give the plant a healthy start in April.

Wildflowers

Wildflowers look beautiful and attract helpful wildlife, including bees, which are drawn to the flowers' nectar and pollen. The flowers come in seed or plugs (*see* page 96), which should be planted on the plot as soon as you buy them. Favourites include cowslip, yarrow, cornflower, foxglove and bird's foot trefoil: a low-growing native perennial with pea-like yellow flowers from May to September, which prefers dry, alkaline soils.

French Marigold

French marigold is a true multitasker. First, it looks pretty. Second, as a companion plant (*see* page 137) it puts off aphids and third, it gives a challengingly bitter edge to the taste of salads. The flower is not too fussy on soil type but is hot on location on the allotment: the sunnier the better. Keep French marigolds off the plot until the last of the frost, watch out for slugs and stake the tallest flowers.

Nasturtium

This is another companion plant that goes down a treat on the dining room table. On the plot, these colourful ground-covering annuals attract insects whose larvae eat aphids, while the flower's scent draws blackfly away from vegetables and hoverflies adore the orange flowers scrambling alongside paths or edging beds. On the table, nasturtium's peppery taste makes it an exotic, tangy garnish or gives a challenging edge when chopped into soured cream or butter.

Companion Planting

Flowers make great companion plants (*see* page 137), but so do vegetables and herbs. Onions, for example, and garlic in particular first confuse then deter pests with their pungent sulphur scent. Mint repels a gaggle of pests, including cabbage white larvae, aphids and flea beetles, while oregano is a total turn-off for cabbage butterflies. Lavender, on the other hand, like other aromatics, exudes chemicals, the pungency of which is too much for many pests to stomach.

checklist

- **When choosing fruit trees, check you have enough space:** Even dwarf trees put on a fair amount of spread and a half-standard tree can stand at over 1 m (3 ft) high.

- **Fruit production peaks in a tree's mid-maturity:** Expect your fruit tree to hit peak performance at around 10 years old.

- **Apple trees are best planted in the dormant season:** Dig them into the ground between November and spring, but avoid planting in frozen soil.

- **Buy soft fruit plants from a reliable source such as a good nursery:** Check to see if the plant comes with a virus-free certificate.

- **Blackcurrants are deemed one of the most nutritious fruits:** The berries are packed with antioxidants and vitamin C.

- **Grapevines can grow in most soils as long as the earth is not prone to waterlogging:** A warm, sheltered suntrap on your allotment could be just the spot.

- **Flowers like a sunny place on the plot, with shelter:** This will spare them a buffeting wind and you the job of staking them for protection.

Vegetables
and Herbs

The Onion Family

Onions featured in the diets of ancient Egyptians and Romans, while the humble onion's place in modern history has been secured by the allotment, for which the vegetable is a staple crop. It is also a boon to our health, containing antioxidants and reducing cholesterol levels in the body. The onion requires little maintenance and is easy to grow from seed or 'sets', which are tiny immature onions. The latter are even easier to grow than seed and are less time consuming.

Onion Types

Onions can be divided into several groups depending on their size, shape and colour. Bulbs can have brown, yellow or red outer skins and can be planted in spring to harvest in late summer. Japanese hybrid onions can be planted to overwinter and harvest in spring. Other common types of onion include shallots, smaller, more elongated and sought after by cooks, bunched spring – now called salad – onions, and pickling varieties, which are mini onions, and are lifted when small.

Onion

Onions should be planted 30 cm (1 ft) apart from each other in well-drained sunny soil in early spring or autumn. Plant with the tips sticking out and cover with netting to thwart pecking birds. Hoe weeds between rows and water if very dry, and avoid splashing the leaves.

 Harvest: Pick when the foliage turns yellow, dry them out on newspaper and store in a cool, dry place.

Shallot

Shallots, smaller, milder and sweeter than onions, are easier to grow from sets, mature faster and store for longer. Like onions, they enjoy a fertile, well-drained neutral or slightly alkaline soil and can be planted closer together in mid-spring. Watch out for onion fly or downy mildew (see page 176) in damp conditions.

Harvest: Lift shallots with a small fork in midsummer and on a dry day and store like onions.

Spring Onion

Spring onions are similar to Japanese onions, but the latter have a slightly stronger flavour and do not produce bulbs. Both are grown the same way, which is on a sunny site with well-draining soil. Sow seedlings 1 cm ($\frac{1}{2}$ in) apart from March and leave them to it.

Harvest: Pick when the onions are the size of pencils before they become too coarse or go to seed.

Garlic

Garlic is fairly easy to grow and is remarkably hardy. Buy a head of garlic from a garden centre – but not a supermarket – break it into segments and plant them upright just below the soil surface in autumn or winter. Choose part of the plot that drains well and catches the sun.

Harvest: Lift the garlic in summer, dry them in the sun or a shed and keep a few to plant next year.

Leek

Leeks, like chives, are also members of the onion family and love humus-rich soil that is neither too wet nor too compacted. They are easy to grow and are great for allotment beginners. Sow in seed trays in late winter and transplant to the plot bed when they are pencil sized.

Harvest: Lift with a fork and store in a coldframe or shed for about two weeks.

Chive

Chives are tough, easy to grow and with their purple pompom flowers make a terrific edge to an allotment bed. In return they like humus-rich and moist soil in full sunlight. Sow in drills from around March, spaced 30 cm (1 ft) apart, and watch them germinate a month later.

Harvest: Cut the long leaves with scissors about 5 cm (2 in) above the soil level, but leave a few leaves for the plant to regrow.

Welsh Onion

This hardy perennial used to grace many cottage gardens and looks like oversized chives with white flowers in summer. The plant likes well-drained soil and full sunshine, and slugs like it too. Seeds can be grown under glass, then planted in rows around April or May, spaced 20 cm (8 in) apart. Not a native of Wales, the name comes from the Old English *welisc*, meaning foreign.

The Cabbage Family

The cabbage–patch gang are all brassicas, be they Brussels sprouts, broccoli or kale. They are all hungry crops, needing rich, fertile, firm soil with the pH scale tilting towards alkaline. Many are sown into a specially prepared seedbed and transplanted five or six weeks later, but they should not be grown in the same place each year and, ideally, they should follow legumes – the so-called 'fixers' such as beans or peas that feed nitrogen into the earth.

How to Grow Brassicas

Both seedbeds and permanent beds on the allotment should be prepared in autumn with well-rotted manure or compost, but brace yourself for serious digging: brassica roots can penetrate below 2m (6½ ft). Also be prepared for pests and diseases, which include clubroot (see page 175), cabbage white caterpillars, cabbage root fly, downy mildew, whitefly, aphids and birds.

Cabbage

Cabbage takes up a lot of space on the allotment but is not hard to maintain and is comfortable in the cooler climates of northern Europe. Bad summers: no problem. Different cabbages can be grown throughout the year in good soil. Cover with fleece if pests swoop and surround with collars to deter cabbage root fly (see page 168).

Harvest: Cut the heads with a sharp knife. You can store red or winter white cabbage for two or three months.

Brussels Sprout

Sadly for the sprout, Christmas comes but once a year. The lucky allotment gardener, however, has from October to March to pluck them from the plant. A hardy vegetable, the sprout can take temperatures of -10°C (14 °F) and can be planted out from May, spaced 70 cm (2¼ ft) apart.

 Harvest: The smaller the sprout the tastier it is, picked from the bottom up; you can freeze the sprout after blanching.

Kale

This vitamin-packed frilly-leaved beauty is perhaps the easiest brassica to grow. Kale does better in a sunny spot and with a mulch of half-rotted compost. It will do even better if you can string up nets before the pigeons swoop.

 Harvest: Cut leaves from several plants at once and harvest often to encourage constant young growth and a long cropping season.

Cauliflower

This is a little harder to grow than other brassicas, but the taste of summer, autumn or winter cauliflower is worth the effort. Winter types are the hardest because they take so long to mature – almost a year. Cauliflower needs fertile, humus-rich soil, even more alkaline than that favoured by other brassicas.

 Harvest: Squeeze the heads before cutting to see if they are firm and cut them in the morning.

Broccoli

Two forms include sprouting broccoli with small florets, or stems, and calabrese, which has one large floret and is quicker to grow than the sprouting alternative. Both like the sun, but calabrese needs plenty of watering to keep it from going woody, while sprouting broccoli needs staking in autumn.

 Harvest: Cut the stems when they are 15 cm (6 in) long but do not strip the plant or let it flower or growth will stop. Store in a plastic bag in the refrigerator for two days or blanch and freeze.

Did You Know?

'Brocco' means sprout in Italian and broccoli was first cultivated by the Romans.

Oriental Greens

There are many types of oriental greens such as mizuna, komatsuna and pak choi, and they should be planted on an open site with partial shade. Dig in well-rotted manure and space 15 cm (6 in) apart. Growing under fleece will protect the crop from beetles and root fly. Remove pests with your fingers or wash the leaves with soapy water.

 Harvest: Pick the leaves when they are small and tender to encourage regrowth, and eating on the day is recommended as the leaves soon wilt.

Kohlrabi

Also called stem cabbage, kohlrabi should be sown indoors and transplanted in rows 30 cm (1 ft) apart when the last frosts are over. Plant in rich, well-drained soil and in full sun.

Harvest: Pull up the plants when the bulbs are tennis-ball sized and store in boxes of sand or sawdust.

Beans, Peas and Corn

Pod vegetables, or legumes, stand alone from all other vegetable groups on the allotment. For these are the nitrogen 'fixers' that draw the gaseous element from the air and pass it into the soil through root nodules. While few things beat the taste of a freshly picked pea from the allotment, nothing beats the soil-enriching qualities of legumes. This makes them ideal in a crop rotation, helping to give tired soil a badly needed nitro-fillip in time for the greedy brassicas next in line.

Peas and Beans

One you've popped a pea from its pod and put it into your mouth, never again will the frozen alternative do, and by growing different types you can enjoy fresh pods from May to October. Mangetout and sugar snaps are easier to grow than standard peas, but don't be put off having a pea. The broad bean, meanwhile, is the oldest of all cultivated beans, dating back to the Stone Age.

Peas

Never sow peas in cold, wet soil and choose a spot that catches plenty of sun before planting in a trench, 8 cm (3 in) apart. The first crop sown from March will be ready in about 12 weeks. Water in dry spells and support the peas on twiggy sticks, keeping an eye out for pea moth.

Harvest: Pick regularly and go for pods that are fresh, green and have not started to dry out. Freeze them, if you must, after blanching.

Broad Beans

Broad beans are the first of the legumes to mature in the year and with follow-up spring sowings can provide produce from June to September. Cover the plants with cloches in cold weather and stake taller plants that need support. Pinching out the tops will help reduce blackfly colonies.

Harvest: Cut the beans off with scissors when pods are about 8 cm (3 in) long and cook them whole. Shell and put in the refrigerator or blanch and freeze.

Runner Beans

Runner beans don't have to be tough and stringy. Sow seeds in alkaline soil from late May to late June, 20 cm (8 in) apart, and make a bamboo ridge or wigwam support for them. Ensuring the soil is constantly moist and doesn't dry out is a key to success, but watch out for slugs and blackfly.

Harvest: Pick when the pods are 15 cm (6 in) long and before the beans inside begin to swell. Store in a cool place for a couple of days or slice, blanch and freeze in plastic bags.

Did You Know?

You can buy stringless cultivars of runner bean, such as 'Desiree' and dwarf cultivars like 'Hestia' that can grow quite happily without supports.

French Bean

French beans are good on an allotment where space is tight and there are two main types, dwarf bush and climbers. The main sowing period is May and June; and the bush types should not need supporting. Water well and mulch in dry periods to keep the soil moist.

 Harvest: Begin picking the pods when they are 10 cm (4 in) long, young and tender and pick often to encourage more pods to form.

Soya Bean

Until recently, soya beans were not reliable in the UK, but with new cultivars such as 'Ustie' they have been bred to suit the British climate. The plant produces downy pods through autumn and can be sown outside in well-drained but moist earth in sunlight once the soil has warmed up in late spring. Hoe around plants regularly and keep them well watered.

 Harvest: Pick when the leaves start falling off, leaving hanging pods from late September. Beans can be stored in airtight containers, but must be boiled before eating to destroy inhibitors for protein ingestion (in other words, in order to gain the maximum protein content from the beans, they should be heated).

Lablab

This ornamental climber produces edible pods and fragrant, sweet pea-like pink flowers. Sow indoors and move outside in late spring or early summer and plant in well-drained soil in a sheltered spot. Train plants up bamboo canes or wires as you would sweet peas or runner beans.

 Harvest: Harvest pods regularly when small, as old, mature pods can become stringy.

Adzuki Bean

Adzuki, which can be used for bean sprouts, produces yellow flowers followed by clusters of smooth, short pods. Seeds are best sown directly outside from May to July but they need well-prepared, well-drained soil. Add a little general fertilizer at sowing time and again when flowers start to appear. Keep well watered during hot, dry periods. Plants are short and often do not need support, but keep them well watered in dry periods.

Harvest: Young tender pods can be harvested like green beans. The entire plant with dry pods still attached may be pulled up and stacked in a dry, well-ventilated place to dry.

Sweetcorn

Sweetcorn, not a legume, is not the easiest crop to grow on allotments but newer cultivars are proving better for the climates of northern Europe. It needs sunlight and shelter from wind. In mild areas you can sow seed directly outside from late May in soil prewarmed for two weeks with cloches or clear plastic. Stake sweetcorn to protect against wind and water well in dry weather.

Harvest: Squeeze a grain and if a watery liquid squirts out it is unripe; a thicker, creamier liquid is a sign the cob is ready. Twist the ripe cob from the stem. To freeze, blanch and pack in foil and plastic bags.

Root and Stem Vegetables

Root vegetables have always been considered the mainstay of the allotment, some being left in the ground until needed, others being lifted and stored in boxes. This hardy breed is the stuff of summer surpluses and the saviour from winter shortages. It comes as no surprise to learn the potato has been cultivated for thousands of years; but more surprising perhaps that it took until the late 1500s to make its way from South America to European shores.

Root Causes

Only the very hardiest root and stem vegetable can be left in the soil or open air without deteriorating, being damaged by the frost or munched by mice. Jerusalem artichokes, parsnips and celeriac pass the test but even they can do with a layer of straw or dead leaves. Swedes, turnips and carrots can tolerate fair amounts of frost, but it is often easier – and a good deal more pleasant – to lift and store in boxes in milder weather than to don boots and dig them out of muddy ground when it's colder.

Harvesting Tip

Easy to grow, potatoes can be tricky to harvest. When you fork them out of the ground, it is not unusual to impale one of the tubers, so slide the fork into the ground around 20 cm (8 in) from the main stem and gently ease them out . Any that you slice should be separated – if they go into storage they will rot and infect the healthy potatoes.

How to Store

Golden rules for storage include:

Store root vegetables in a box, tub or tin and in layers separated with sand, soil or peat.

 Throw away damaged or diseased vegetables as they can taint healthy crops.

 Handle the vegetables carefully – even minor bruises can lead to rot.

 Rub off mud, remove leaves, store in a cool place and inspect frequently.

Potatoes

Potatoes are perfect fodder for the allotment, not only because they are easy to grow, but because they offer good ground cover to keep out weeds. The only thing holding you back on choice is your imagination. There are hundreds of types, all different in size and colour, texture and flavour. Skins can be red, yellow, brown or purple and textures can range from light and fluffy to heavy and waxy.

Class Act

Potatoes are classed as 'earlies', 'second earlies' and 'maincrops' depending on how long it takes them to mature – 14 to 16 weeks for the earlies and up to 18 to 20 weeks for the maincrops. Examples include:

 First Earlies: 'Epicure' – hardy, round and white; 'Orla' – pale yellow and blight resistant.

 Second Earlies: 'Maris Piper'– waxy flesh, creamy taste; 'Charlotte' – slug resistant.

 Maincrops: 'Ratte' – salad potato; King Edward – good baker, susceptible to blight.

Sourcing Potatoes

Regardless of the type of potato you want to grow, you should buy stock only from reputable sources like nurseries. Avoid trying to grow potatoes from ones bought at the supermarket, which have not been specially bred to be sprouted.

Growing Root and Stem Crops

Potatoes

Potatoes – certified free from blight – need sunny, humus-rich and well-drained soil. The earth needs to be worked over with manure or compost and, ideally, have a sprinkling of seaweed meal thrown into the bottom of the trenches. Plant around March and keep the soil moist. In warm, humid weather, spray with fungicide to keep on top of blight.

Harvest: Dig them up on a dry day and leave them in the sun for a couple of hours to dry. Store in a cool, dark place – not too warm or they sprout and not too cold or the starch turns to sugar.

Sweet Potato

Sweet potatoes are popular on allotments in milder areas and kept under cover on plots elsewhere. Plants are ordered as cuttings and should be planted around May in a frost-free, well-lit spot in sandy soil until early June. Well watered, tubers take around four months to mature.

Harvest: Lift the tubers in autumn once the plants have started to die down.

Yam

Put yams on your must-try list on the allotment. It is a vigorous climber, sends out shoots up to 3 m (10 ft) long and can be grown up bamboo canes like runner beans. Plant small tubers outside at the end of May in a fertile, well-watered and well-drained soil in full sun.

 Harvest: Like sweet potatoes, harvest in autumn as the plants start to die down. Store yams in a cool, dry place.

Turnip

Turnips are easy to grow, quick to mature and can be harvested mature or young. Choose an open site with fertile, well-drained soil. Sow early turnips in February and thin out the quick-growing seedlings when they are 2.5 cm (1 in) high. Water regularly to stop the roots turning woody.

> ## Did You Know?
>
> **You should not grow potatoes near tomatoes as they belong to the same family and may infect each other with disease.**

 Harvest: Pull up turnips from May to September and store in a box, layered in peat substitute.

Swede

Though easy to grow, swedes take over 20 weeks to mature. Sow seeds in rows 40 cm (16 in) apart from March until mid-June and thin out the seedlings when large enough to handle. Water during dry periods but try to keep the soil evenly moist to prevent cracking. Dry roots can lead to a bitter taste.

 Harvest: Lift when the leaves have turned yellow by easing up with a fork. Store in boxes, sandwiched between layers of sand or peat substitute.

Parsnip

Parsnips are easy to grow, need little maintenance and can be left in the soil until needed. Sow in groups of three or four seeds in March or April and thin out when they are about 2.5 cm (1 in) high. Keep the soil evenly moist and look out for carrot fly.

Harvest: The roots are ready to lift when the foliage starts to die down in autumn. To store, remove the leaves and box up in a shed.

Carrot

Give them a sunny, sheltered and warm plot with sandy soil and your carrots will do the rest. You can plant early, maincrop and late varieties, but avoid using fresh manure – carrots hate it. Seed can be stored for up to three years.

Harvest: Use a trowel to lever up without tugging too hard on the tuft, cut off leaves and store between layers of dry peat or sand in a wood box, making sure they do not touch.

Beetroot

Very easy to grow, beetroot needs regular watering on its sun-catching, well-drained bed and can be planted from March to June. Thin out when seedlings are about 5 cm (2 in) tall and keep on watering on a regular pattern or the roots will become woody and split.

Harvest: Pull up and put on their sides in a box of sand and store in a frost-free place.

Radish

Radishes are fast growing and need to be harvested young to ensure they remain succulent. Sow little and often from March to August and keep the soil moist to ensure rapid growth and healthy roots, especially in hotter, drier conditions.

Did You Know?

**Radishes can be used as a 'catch crop' – sown between rows
of slower-growing vegetables such as peas or potatoes.**

 Harvest: Pull radishes as required, ensuring you don't leave them to mature and become woody. Winter cultivars can be left in the ground and dug up as required.

Celery

Celery can be tricky to grow and there are two types: trench – with soil heaped around the stems – and self-blanching – smaller and easier to grow for new allotment holders. Soil must never dry out and seamless growing conditions are required so transplant, harden off and water properly.

 Harvest: Harvest between August and October, before the first frosts. Celery can be frozen if you trim into smaller sections and blanch before freezing.

Celeriac

Also known as turnip-rooted celery, this increasingly popular vegetable is easier to grow than celery. It should be sown from February in pots or trays of compost and planted out in June. Water and mulch the plant in dry weather and remove sideshoots as they form.

 Harvest: Lift from late September or overwinter in the ground, covered with straw or compost. Can be put in the refrigerator for a week or so.

Salsify

This slow-growing root vegetable is popular in southern Europe, has white or black skin and is a real boon on the allotment not only for its taste and exotic status, but because it attracts useful insects. Sow in spring about 30 cm (1 ft) apart in soil that is not over-rich, and keep an eye out for carrot fly.

Harvest: Roots are ready for lifting in spring but can be left in the soil to overwinter. The plant can be cooked like asparagus.

Florence Fennel

This white, aniseed-flavour bulb should be grown in moist soil. Sow the seeds from May to July and, when large enough to handle, thin seedlings to 20 cm (8 in) apart. As the bulbs develop, mound up the soil around them and continue earthing up until the bulb is mature in summer.

 Harvest: Lift mature bulbs as required and use the foliage as a herb garnish.

Jerusalem Artichoke

Plant the small tubers in well-dug and fertilized soil around March or April. Plants need very little care and attention during the growing season and are rarely troubled by pests and diseases. Some allotment holders use the plant as a screen, but it may need support on exposed, windy sites.

 Harvesting: Leave in the ground until needed to keep it firm and then lift the way you would potatoes. Store in the refrigerator for up to a week.

Shoot, Stalk and Bud Vegetables

Make way for the allotment aristocrats. These are the most prized and popular vegetables on the plot and include the globe artichoke, which adds a noble – and pointy – grandeur to the allotment, and asparagus, which is one of the oldest cultivated vegetables and was enjoyed by the Romans. Being a perennial, the vegetable can stay in the ground for well over a decade, which is ideal: few things beat the juicy spears of asparagus in late spring and many allotment holders are happy harvesting this plant year after year.

Different Types

Growing white asparagus is harder than green, so perhaps first-time allotment holders should consider softening themselves up on the green varieties. These contain more vitamins and are held up by many people as being tastier. The cardoon, meanwhile, is a relative of the artichoke, but it is the stalks rather than the head that are eaten, and some people feel the taste of the former cannot match the deliciousness of the latter.

Fruit or Vegetable?

Another stem plant, rhubarb, is considered a fruit but the plant that originated in Mongolia is in fact a vegetable. Like asparagus, it is a perennial and, like asparagus, it is fairly easy to grow, but there are differences to consider when it comes to sowing, growing and harvesting the two plants.

Growing Shoot, Stalk and Bud Vegetables

Asparagus

Asparagus is not difficult to grow if kept well fed and weed-free, and much of its cultural mystique is not matched by its methods of cultivation. Given enough space, each crown can yield over a dozen spears in the cutting season. Asparagus can be raised from seed, which takes a long time, or from young dormant plants called crowns.

- **Planting:** It is the one-year-old crowns that many allotment gardeners choose to grow, planting them in March or April. Make a ridge along the middle of the trench, put the crowns on top and spread out the roots. Fill in the trench, water and mulch with manure or compost. Weed the beds by hand – but not by hoe, which could damage the shallow roots – and apply fertilizer in spring.
- **Harvest:** The season for cutting asparagus runs from April to late June and you should harvest when the spears are 15 cm (6 in) long. Snip the spears 4 cm (1½ in) below the soil, but make a clean cut to encourage continuous cropping.

Did You Know?

You should avoid harvesting asparagus for the first two years and in the third year pick from mid-April for six weeks and in subsequent years for eight weeks.

Globe Artichokes

Globe artichokes reach up to 1.8 m (6 ft) high and can be used on the plot for screening other plants. The vegetable, grown from seed or young plants, offers its best heads in the second year of cropping and becomes more prolific thereafter. Sow the

seeds in rich, well-fed soil in March or April and space them around 70 cm (2¼ ft) apart. The plants need little upkeep once established but they dislike cold, damp conditions as much as they do slugs, blackfly and greenfly.

Harvest: Cut the stem with secateurs 10 cm (4 in) below the flower head from July to October but before the artichoke starts to flower.

Rhubarb

Rhubarb prefers full sun but is fairly easy going and can tolerate acidy soils after a healthy forking over with manure. You should plant rhubarb in an open bed on the allotment away from the shade of trees. The plant can be grown from seed but most plot holders choose a crown, or set, as their starting point. Plant out in autumn around 1 m (3 ft) apart. As long as you keep the plants moist in summer and dry in winter, it should look after itself without needing too much attention.

Harvest: Twist, but don't cut, the plant at its base, choosing the thickest stalks first. Rhubarb can be frozen, so cut into smaller sections and put straight in the freezer.

Cucumbers and Squashes

Cucumber, marrow and courgette, squash and pumpkin all belong to the gourd or *Cucurbitaceae* family, and all will bring flesh and substance to your plot. Courgette, also called zucchini, has a more delicate flavour than marrow, while pumpkin and squash are easy to grow. Their shapes, sizes and colour are almost always guaranteed to trigger a fun-loving vibe in the doughtiest of plot holders as they come to harvest these quintessential icons of the allotment, autumn and Halloween.

Cucumbers

Cucumbers, thought to have originated in India, are best grown under glass, but you can also buy cultivars for outdoor growing, which are rougher-skinned. The plant likes a sheltered, sunny spot and very rich soil, so dig in compost or manure. Being tender plants, cucumbers should not be planted outside until early summer. Start planting your outdoor cucumber seeds in late spring, but keep them indoors. Harden off by taking the plants outside for extended periods before finally planting out in early summer. They must be watered regularly throughout summer and fed weekly with comfrey tea or tomato feed.

Harvest: Plants produce about a dozen cucumbers each, which should be cut carefully with a knife or secateurs mid- to late-summer before they start to yellow.

Courgettes and Marrows

Courgettes and marrows like sunny beds protected from wind and a moist soil, but be warned, courgettes grow really fast and can fruit for several weeks. Sow them outdoors from late May where they will germinate in a few days. Feed with potassium-rich fertilizer and watch out for slugs.

 Harvest: Pick courgettes and marrows when the fruit is quite small; store in a cool, dry place.

Pumpkins and Squashes

Sunny, sheltered plots with well-drained, humus-rich soil make a good home for these vegetables. Sow outdoors from June, but cover with cloches if the weather is still cold. Keep well watered and mulched, feed with liquid seaweed if leaves go yellow and look out for slugs.

Harvest: Pumpkins and winter squashes can be left to mature on the plant, but remove them before the first frost strikes. Store larger fruits in a frost-free area.

Melons

This tender annual needs warmth and a humus-rich, well-drained soil. In cooler climates, melons should be grown in a frame or under cloches. Sow in early spring for under-glass crops and mid-spring for outdoor crops. Let outdoor melons form four fruit, greenhouse melons six.

Harvest: Early cultivars ripen from midsummer, later ones early autumn. When melons are ready to be harvested, they give off a strong smell, crack and soften around the stalk. Store in the refrigerator for a few days.

Did You Know?

Spraying with soft soap can help cucumbers ward off mosaic virus, which is one of the most common plant viruses, causing yellow mottling, distorted leaves and stunted growth.

Tender Vegetables

Being native to South America, tomatoes have endured their stay in the cooler climes of northern Europe remarkably well. Since they were introduced into Britain in the sixteenth century, tomatoes have risen steadily in esteem and in recent years probably more hours have been devoted on the allotment to fine-tuning the successful cultivation of this plant than lots of other edible produce. Other tender but tenacious plants that have made the allotment their home include peppers, chillies and aubergines.

Tomato Types

Fresh from the vine, their taste is divine. Tomatoes come in numerous cultivars and types from the minuscule cherry to the lush plum and the outrageously bulbous beefsteak tomato. You can grow yellow, orange, green and purple tomatoes, and you can raise them from tall standard varieties down to bush or hanging-basket types.

Different Tomato Varieties
Different types of tomato include:

- **Vine:** Also known as the cordon or the indeterminate, the vine tomato is popular with growers and dangles fruit off shoots from a main stem that needs support such as a stake.
- **Bush:** These tomatoes grow into compact plants, which are easier to control than vines. But all the fruit tends to ripen at the same time, so forward planning is important to avoid gluts.

Semi-determinate: This cross between a vine and bush tomato grows into a straggly plant form that requires a frame.

 Tumbling: These mini plants yield cherry tomatoes.

Growing Tender Vegetables

Tomato

Grow bags are often used for tomatoes but can take more looking after than those grown in pots or the ground. Sow in seed trays or small pots and transplant to larger pots when leaves start to form. Sow outdoors in late March in a sunny, sheltered spot, and support with a bamboo cane as the plant grows. Remove sideshoots, water regularly and feed with liquid comfrey weekly. Climbing types should be spaced 45 cm (1½ ft) apart and bush tomatoes 60 cm (2 ft). Mulch and cover with fleece.

 Harvest: Start picking by hand when the fruit is ripe and fully coloured. At the end of the season, lay unripe fruit in one layer on a tray and leave in a shed to ripen.

Did You Know?

Putting a banana, apple or pear among tomatoes can speed up ripening of the tomatoes as these three fruits emit ethylene gas.

Pepper and Chilli

Growing sweet and chilli peppers on the plot is increasing in popularity. Both are grown in a similar way to tomatoes, but chillies are easier to nurture. They grow best under glass but also do well in a sheltered suntrap outside. Being more exotic than most vegetables, they need rich, moist soil and are best started off under cloches, spaced 30 cm (1 ft) apart. Water but not too much and watch out for a host of pests and diseases: botrytis, red spider mite, whitefly and aphids.

Harvest: Pick chillies when they are ripe and glossy for immediate use, drying, pickling or freezing them; cut peppers – don't pick - from the plant, leaving a small stem on the fruit.

Aubergine

Aubergines are grown like tomatoes and new cultivars are more suited to northern European climates. Although they can be grown outside, aubergines are better off in a frame unless the summer is good. Plant outside from late May in well-drained soil. They need high-potash fertilizer and plenty of water, feeding and staking as the fruits develop.

Harvest: Cut each fruit close to the stem from August when they have grown about 20 cm (8 in) long and are a rich and shiny deep purple. Store for a couple of weeks in the refrigerator.

Okra

Okra, also called ladies' fingers or gumbo, thrives in temperatures over 20°C (68°F). Try growing in the allotment greenhouse or outside when the weather is hot enough, but avoid shifting from one to the other as okra dislikes being moved. Keep seedlings on the dry side but mulch the soil. Okra usually grows well in any good soil, but once the first flowers are formed feed weekly.

Harvest: The pods should be cut with a knife or secateurs while tender and just under 10 cm (4 in) long from July through to October. They must be picked often – at least every other day or yields will decrease. Also, if the okra gets too large, it will be tough and stringy. Okra plants have short hairs that may irritate bare skin, so wear gloves and long sleeves.

Lettuce and Salads

Lettuce has never been more popular. It can be grown full-sized with billowing heads, or as leaves that can be cut from a stem to give second, third or even fourth crops from the original sowing. This so-called cut-and-come-again technique can yield an astonishing weight of leaf from one tiny piece of land, which makes it such a winner on the allotment. The burgeoning popularity of TV cookery shows and the ubiquitous presence of celebrity chefs have helped up the status of more exotic culinary curios like radicchio. This has filtered down to the allotment, coaxing growers to push boundaries and bring a little bit of rock 'n' roll to their plot.

Lettuce

There are two types of lettuce: those that produce hearts and foliage-only, non-heart lettuces. To keep a family stocked up on lettuce from late spring to autumn, try small sowings at weekly intervals in April and May, and again in August, cutting each crop two or three times.

Lettuce Types

You can choose from many lettuces, including:

 Butterhead: A well-known lettuce, this has soft floppy leaves and has a long season.

Crisphead or 'Iceberg': This tightly structured lettuce exudes freshness and has a very crisp texture.

Cos: This includes the well-known 'Little Gem', which is small, sweet and quick to mature.

Looseleaf: These have no hearts but curled leaves and can be picked over a long time.

Growing Lettuce

Lettuce likes full sun, especially in spring and autumn, though summer crops can do with cooling off in afternoon shade. It likes well-drained, slightly alkaline soil with plenty of manure or compost. Sow outside from March through to September, and watch out for slugs, aphids and downy mildew (*see page 176*).

Harvest: Pick non-hearting lettuce by cutting leaves near ground level and leaving the stump to regrow for three or four weeks before a return sweep with the scissors. Harvest hearted lettuce when firm and ripe, early in the morning while the leaves are still moist.

Salads

Rocket

A darling of the 1990s salad bowl, rocket can mature in as little as four weeks but runs to seed quickly. Frequent sowing and harvesting therefore will be in the offing. The plant likes a sheltered spot with fairly fertile soil, can be sown from March to September and should be watered if dry.

Harvest: Pick the leaves often when they are young and tender to encourage new growth, but always leave a few leaves on the plant. Remove seed heads, which will stop growth.

Chervil

This tender herb has pretty, delicate leaves that look like parsley and can self-seed. It prefers partial shade and should be sown directly on to moist, rich soil from spring to midsummer. Thin out the seedlings after two or three weeks and water well in dry weather.

✓ **Harvest**: Pick leaves about two months after sowing. You cannot dry chervil, but you can freeze it.

Chicory, Endive and Radicchio

These three different plants are forms of chicory and should be planted in moist, well-manured soil on an open site that catches full or partial sunlight. Pale-leafed chicory and endive should be planted early to midsummer, while purple-leafed radicchio can go in a little earlier. Water the plants regularly but avoid nitrogen-rich fertilizer, which can cause the leaves to rot.

✓ **Harvest**: Pick six to eight weeks after sowing by cutting the heads with a sharp knife at ground level. Store in the refrigerator for a few days.

Spinach

Spinach is fairly easy to grow but needs regular watering. Find a lightly shaded spot on the allotment that has nitrogen-rich soil and sow every two or three weeks from early spring. Winter-hardy crops can be grown as late as autumn.

✓ **Harvest**: Treat as a cut-and-come-again vegetable, cutting off leaves with scissors or picking them off with your fingers when the leaves are young and tender. Store in the refrigerator for a couple of days.

Chard

Chard is a good alternative to spinach, is easy to grow and largely free from pests and diseases. Like spinach, it thrives on a nitrogen-packed soil when it comes to be sown in late spring in mild weather. Chard needs closer attention when young and may need feeding if the soil is poor.

✓ **Harvest**: Pick before they become too large and harvest throughout autumn and winter.

Purslane

Purslane is a handy cut-and-come-again crop that can be used as a filler for that odd corner of your allotment in need of a crop. Sown little and often from early summer, purslane needs regular watering and weeding, but is mostly free from pest and disease trouble.

Harvest: Pick the leaves often when they are young and tender to encourage new growth.

Mustard Greens

Another cut-and-come-again crop, this Oriental brassica needs nitro-rich fertile soil with plenty of moisture. Sow into the soil from late spring onwards, but not too early or the plant may bolt, and water regularly.

Harvest: Use scissors to cut the leaves about 2 cm (¾ in) from the base when they are about 10 cm (4 in) high.

Dandelion

Dandelions have been used for many centuries as a healing herb and food. They are prolific growers, as any allotment holder will tell you, and this is one crop where failure is all but impossible. You can buy seeds or collect them yourself in early to late summer. For a bumper crop, dig in some well-rotted manure or compost on a sunny spot and then scatter the seed.

Harvest: Cut the leaves with scissors, store in a cool, dry place or the refrigerator and use within a week.

Herbs

Herbs are the spice of the allotment holder's life. They are delicate and pretty, functional and aromatic. You can dot them around your plot to fill nooks and corners or you can use them for edging that is both decorative and practical. The heady scents of some of them will be as pleasing to you as they are repellent to a few of the unwanted pests on your plot, and because they are not needed in large quantities these small plants rarely take up much of your time, but herbs always bring a sensual twist to the allotment.

Choosing Herbs

Herbs are among the easiest crops to grow, require little attention and will flourish as long as they are planted in the right place. Some love the sun, others prefer shade to keep their delicate leaves tender. When choosing herbs, think of the ones you like and the conditions they will need to grow comfortably.

Different Types

Herbs can be divided into three groups. Annuals include basil, chervil, parsley and dill, and can be planted when the soil is warm enough in late spring. Herbaceous herbs take in chives and mint, while evergreens include bay, rosemary, thyme and sage.

Did You Know?

Annual herbs are great planted among vegetables as they can deter pests, while perennials need their own space like a herb bed.

Mint

Mint likes damp but well-drained and humus-rich soil in sun or partial shade. Plant 30 cm (1 ft) apart but take care, it can run riot and take over the herb bed. Caterpillars, aphids and carrot flies (see pages 168–69) are said to dislike mint.

 Harvest: Cut 20 cm (8 in) long stems before the plant flowers: freezing locks in the flavour more than drying.

Rosemary

This scented bush should be planted in a well-drained, sunny spot outside after the danger of frost has passed. Rosemary should be clipped back to keep it compact and it can be used on the allotment as a plant boundary.

 Harvest: Cut sprigs in early summer when the narrow, pointy leaves are tender and use or hang upside down to dry.

Thyme

A Mediterranean herb, thyme needs light, well-drained soil in full sunlight. Different types include creeping to upright thyme and you should trim bushes after flowering to encourage new growth.

 Harvest: Pick and use or dry, or you can add it to lavender to repel moths.

Sage

Sage can easily be propagated from cuttings and its soft velvety leaves make it attractive on the plot, but it does not like heavy soils, so plant in full sun and well-draining earth. Sage repels slugs, aphids and caterpillars.

 Harvest: Pick throughout the year, dry on a rack in a well-ventilated area and store in airtight tubs.

Russian Tarragon

There are two sorts of aniseed-like tarragon. French is more prized, while Russian is hardier and easier to grow. Russian is more vigorous and can tolerate poorer soils. It does not need lots of attention and can be grown from seed.

 Harvest: Sprigs can be harvested about 10 weeks after planting and throughout the summer months.

French Tarragon

Like mint, French tarragon relies on underground rhizomes to spread and can colonize beds. It cannot be propagated from seed so buy a plant or snip off a scrap of rhizome, then plant it in a well-drained bed.

Harvest: Cut regularly and wrap freshly cut sprigs in a perforated polythene bag to refrigerate for a few days.

Oregano and Marjoram

Oregano, marjoram and pot marjoram like sunny spots on the allotment and dry soil that drains well. Sow the seeds in trays in spring, thin out seedlings and plant out. Divide clumps in spring for new growth.

 Harvest: Cut stems above the lowest set of leaves from June to August while flowering.

Basil

Harden off basil seeds before planting on the allotment after the frosts, spaced 20 cm (8 in) apart. Mulch with compost and try to avoid splashing the leaves when you water the plant. Basil does not like the cold, damp, humidity or slugs.

> ✅ **Harvest:** Pick leaves weekly to promote more growth and prevent from flowering. Do not dry or freeze.

Dill

Feathery-leaved dill thrives in moist soil and can grow to 1 m (3 ft) high. Sow into beds from March to June and keep well watered. Avoid planting dill close to fennel, as the two are so similar they may cross breed and lose their distinctive qualities.

> ✅ **Harvest:** Using scissors, clip the foliage throughout the season.

Fennel

Sow seeds in spring or autumn around 60 cm (2 ft) apart in a sunny spot with fertile soil. Or you can use a piece of root from an established plant, but take care; fennel will scatter seed everywhere unless you snip off the flower heads.

> ✅ **Harvest:** Use scissors to clip the tall fern-like foliage and store in a cool, dry place.

Parsley

Parsley grows from spring to autumn and comes with curly milder-flavoured leaves or flat leaves. Plant seeds outdoors from about three weeks after the last frosts in well-drained ground that offers partial shade. Look out for slugs, aphids and carrot flies.

> ✅ **Harvest:** Pick until flowers start to appear in the plant's second year and use or freeze.

Summer Savory

Sow summer savory seeds in a sunny spot in open ground from April to June about 20 cm (8 in) apart. Thin the annual seedlings when they are large enough. You can also sow evergreen winter savory seeds in a sunny, well-drained position in late spring or autumn.

 Harvest: Use summer or winter savory leaves fresh or dry them.

Lemon Grass

The strongly scented lemon grass has cane-like stems and likes a moderately humid atmosphere and moisture-retaining soil. Allotment holders will probably need a greenhouse or protected container such as a loose polythene bag with ventilation holes.

 Harvest: Cut the stems at ground level with scissors or secateurs.

Coriander

Grow coriander on well-drained soil in a sunny spot, the drier the better. It does not like damp or humid conditions and when the plant has matured stake it for support with thin sticks. Planted with brassicas, coriander confuses cabbage mealy aphids.

 Harvest: Pick the leaves when young and tender and dry out seeds before storing in an airtight box.

Borage

Borage is another rampant spreader so, unless kept in check, expect to see carpets of the coarse leaves and blue flowers on your allotment. You can broadcast the seed (scatter them by hand) in spring on open ground and thin out to around 30 cm (1 ft) apart.

 Harvest: Pick just before use, as the leaves wilt quickly and lose their flavour fairly rapidly when dried.

Bay

Though this small evergreen is usually grown in containers, it can be raised on the open plot and reach quite a height. It needs full sunlight, protection from winds and well-drained soil. However, it can also tolerate mediocre soils.

 Harvest: Cut the leaves and use fresh or store in a dark place so the leaves keep their colour.

Season's End

Herbs add small splashes of colour and interest to the allotment, but don't lose sight of the bigger picture. At the end of the season there's plenty to do before calling it a day, closing the allotment gate and walking home to put your feet up in front of the fire. In autumn you can:

- **Fork summer compost on the beds and gather up leaves for the leaf-mould bin.**
- **Disconnect downpipes to water butts to prevent them from overflowing.**
- **Ensure plant stakes are firmly in the ground and tied securely but not too tightly to stems.**
- **Clean up; tidy out shed, oil tools, wash pots and clear up the compost heap.**

Latin Names

Every fruit, vegetable and flower mentioned in the *Green Guide: Allotment Gardening* has a Latin name. Peas, for example, are *Pisum sativum*, which looks terrifying when you are not used to this all-but-forgotten language, but the two words mean nothing more than your first and last names, except the other way round: in the plant world, the last name comes first. And just like the Smiths down the road, endive, chicory and radicchio belong to the same family, *Chichorium*. The second Latin name tells you a little about the plant, so pumpkin, *Curcubito maxima*, gives you an indication this plant is a big one. Down on the allotment, Latin is not dead, it is a growing language.

Checklist

 The onion is an easy-to-grow allotment staple: The family includes garlic, shallots and chives.

 Cabbages, broccoli and cauliflower are all brassicas: They are ideally suited to the cooler climate of northern Europe.

 Root and stem vegetables are the mainstay of the allotment: Some can be left in the ground until needed, while others can be lifted and stored in boxes.

 Asparagus and globe artichoke are allotment aristocrats: They are among the most prized and popular vegetables on the plot.

 Pumpkins and squashes can be fed with liquid seaweed: Perk them up with a quick feed if leaves start to turn yellow.

 You can grow all kinds of tomatoes: From minuscule cherry to bulbous beefsteak, yellow-, orange-, green- and purple-coloured tomatoes.

 Herbs have diverse uses: You can dot them around your plot to fill nooks and corners or you can use them for decorative and practical edging.

checklist

Included here are the checklists from the end of each chapter of the book. Use them to remind yourself of what to do. Tick them off as you go along!

The Joy of Allotments

☐ **Allotments have many benefits:** They are good for your health, finances and peace of mind.

☐ **A plot of land of around 30 m (98 ft) long is highly productive:** You can grow fruit and vegetables, herbs and spices, cut flowers and other plants for the home.

☐ **Allotments teach us important lessons in sustainability:** They are among the few remaining havens of wildlife and biodiversity in our cities.

☐ **Working on allotments does wonders for your social life:** You meet like-minded people, share ideas and swap fresh produce.

☐ **Everyone can enjoy working on an allotment:** More young families and even children are discovering the pleasures of spending time on the allotment.

☐ **You can take more control over your food:** Allotments are good if you worry about pesticide and other chemical residues and intensive farming practices.

☐ **You will learn a lot on an allotment:** You can become an expert in hoeing, weeding and planting.

Getting Started

☐ **Where to start**: Your search for an allotment may start at the town hall, library or town information centre.

☐ **It pays to visit sites and talk to plot holders**: Getting on to the site will give you a clearer idea of what you are letting yourself in for.

☐ **Don't lose heart**: Keep phoning up the local authority to impress upon them how keen you are for an allotment now.

☐ **Cost**: The average yearly fee for an allotment is around the £30 mark, and rents are usually collected in one lump at the beginning of the year.

☐ **Size**: Most allotment plots are between 150 sq m (1,614 sq ft) and 250 sq m (2,700 sq ft), with a typical plot laid out at 25 m (82 ft) long and 10 m (33 ft) wide.

☐ **Rules and etiquette**: Allotments are governed by a series of rules, and their close-knit communities rely on a strong code of etiquette.

☐ **How much time will my plot take up?** Ask yourself how much time can I spend and should I spend on the plot?

☐ **Plot characteristics to look out for**: Is your allotment overshadowed by buildings or trees and is it flat or on a slope?

Planning Your Plot

☐ **Get to know your soil**: Rub it between your fingers to see if it is a sandy, silty or clay soil.

☐ **Test your soil's acidity or alkalinity**: Buy an easy-to-use kit from your garden centre to check the pH levels of your soil.

☐ **Choose which vegetables you want**: A good balance between succulent fruits, bulky vegetables and colourful flowers will ensure plenty of variety.

☐ **Select the right plants**: You may want to avoid ones that take up a lot of space, take a long time to grow or produce poor yields.

☐ **Make sure you plan your plot carefully**: Try to design a cohesive and logical layout with easy-to-navigate paths and features.

☐ **Plan an effective crop rotation**: Avoid planting vegetables in exactly the same plot to ensure good harvests and to keep soil-borne pests and diseases at bay.

☐ **Make sure you choose the right permanent structures**: A good shed, greenhouse and compost bin are important to the smooth running of your allotment.

Preparing To Garden

☐ **Get the right tools**: Choosing well will save money in the long run and make your job easier.

☐ **Make sure your soil is rich and healthy**: This is the key to success on the allotment.

☐ **The amount of compost you need varies**: It depends on the condition of your soil, size of the allotment bed and what you want to grow.

☐ **Fertilizers offer plants quick bursts of nutrition**: This can give a real boost to flagging fruit, vegetables and flowers.

☐ **Seeds or plugs**: Allotment holders can grow from traditional seed or buy mini 'plug' plants to avoid having to sow from scratch.

☐ **Plugs are growing in popularity**: Many nurseries and seed companies now sell a wide range of produce including strawberries, cabbages, cauliflowers and lettuce.

☐ **Clearing a plot is one of the hardest jobs**: It is also one of the most rewarding, giving you a glimpse of the challenge ahead.

☐ **There are many alternatives to compost**: These include green manure, leaf mould and worm compost.

Gardening Time

☐ **Planting seed on your allotment is the easiest way of sowing**: All you do is plant it outside and directly into the soil.

☐ **Before sowing, you need to prepare the beds**: Clear the soil of weeds and stones and rake it into a fine tilth.

☐ **Cloches and mini polytunnels protect your plants**: They raise soil and air temperature to extend the growing season and the range of crops.

☐ **When you start transplanting seedlings, work quickly and efficiently**: Seedlings are fragile and their stems and rootballs should be treated carefully.

☐ **You may need to spend around 15 hours a week on the plot**: Jobs include sowing and planting, weeding and watering.

☐ **Weeds are bad in several ways**: They compete with crops for soil nutrients, water and light, and they can host pests.

☐ **An organic allotment can save you money**: It rules out having to buy expensive non-organic chemicals, but it is more time consuming and harder work.

Harvesting Fruit and Vegetables

☐ **Harvesting is one of the most important jobs in the allotment calendar**: It is also one of the most rewarding, when you come to pick the fruits of all your hard work.

☐ **Most plot harvesters find themselves collecting bounty throughout the year**: They have planned what they want to eat and planted accordingly.

☐ **If you are harvesting on a hot summer's day, it might be worth investing in a cool box**: You can pop your most sun-sensitive fruit and vegetables out of the heat to keep them fresh.

☐ **The best place to store produce is somewhere dry, airy and cool**: This will keep your fruit and vegetables free from damp and away from the frost.

☐ **You can bottle your produce in sealed containers**: This is a delicious way of enjoying healthy produce canned straight from the allotment.

☐ **Drying fruit and vegetables can intensify their taste**: Do this at home on trays or in net sacks strung from the ceiling.

Troubleshooting

☐ **There are several ways to reduce the problems caused by pests**: You can rotate your crops, start with healthy crops and grow them well.

☐ **One of the best forms of pest prevention is to check plants at their most vulnerable stage**: Early spring is a great time to get on to the allotment and undertake a thorough pest patrol.

☐ **Plant diseases are caused by bacteria, viruses and fungi**: Telltale signs range from cankers or scabs, black spots, wilting and mildew to malformations and patterned leaves.

☐ **Minimizing the risk of disease on your plot is simple**: Avoid over-watering plants and firming compost too heavily, do not overcrowd plants and encourage good ventilation.

☐ **Be vigilant with weeds**: Weed regularly and frequently to keep on top of the problem.

☐ **Some weeds can prove useful if they are tucked away from the main crops**: Black medick attracts butterflies and bees, while fat hen is a focus for hoverflies.

☐ **Make weeding easier by sowing seeds in straight rows**: You will know for sure anything that comes up between rows must be a weed.

Fruit and Flowers

☐ **When choosing fruit trees, check you have enough space**: Even dwarf trees put on a fair amount of spread and a half-standard tree can stand at over 1 m (3 ft) high.

- [ ] **Fruit production peaks in a tree's mid-maturity:** Expect your fruit tree to hit peak performance at around 10 years old.
- [ ] **Apple trees are best planted in the dormant season:** Dig them into the ground between November and spring, but avoid planting in frozen soil.
- [ ] **Buy soft fruit plants from a reliable source such as a good nursery:** Check to see if the plant comes with a virus-free certificate.
- [ ] **Blackcurrants are deemed one of the most nutritious fruits:** The berries are packed with antioxidants and vitamin C.
- [ ] **Grapevines can grow in most soils as long as the earth is not prone to waterlogging:** A warm, sheltered suntrap on your allotment could be just the spot.
- [ ] **Flowers like a sunny place on the plot, with shelter:** This will spare them a buffeting wind and you the job of staking them for protection.

Vegetables and Herbs

- [ ] **The onion is an easy-to-grow allotment staple:** The family includes garlic, shallots and chives.
- [ ] **Cabbages, broccoli and cauliflower are all brassicas:** They are ideally suited to the cooler climate of northern Europe.
- [ ] **Root and stem vegetables are the mainstay of the allotment:** Some can be left in the ground until needed, while others can be lifted and stored in boxes.
- [ ] **Asparagus and globe artichoke are allotment aristocrats:** They are among the most prized and popular vegetables on the plot.
- [ ] **Pumpkins and squashes can be fed with liquid seaweed:** Perk them up with a quick feed if leaves start to turn yellow.
- [ ] **You can grow all kinds of tomatoes:** From minuscule cherry to bulbous beefsteak, yellow-, orange-, green- and purple-coloured tomatoes.
- [ ] **Herbs have diverse uses:** You can dot them around your plot to fill nooks and corners or you can use them for decorative and practical edging.

Further Reading

Andrews, S., *The Allotment Handbook*,
Eco-Logic Books, 2001

Borish, E. *What Will I Do With All Those Courgettes?*
Fidelio Press, 2002

Bridgewater, A. & G., *The Allotment Specialist*,
New Holland, 2007

Crouch, D.; Ward, C., *The Allotment: Its Landscape and Culture*, Five Leaves Publications, 1997

Crouch, D.; Sempik, J; Wiltshire, R., *Growing in the Community: A Good Practice Guide for the Management of Allotments*, LGA Publications, 2001

Crouch, D., *The Art of Allotments*,
Five Leaves Publications, 2003

Foley, C., *How to Plant Your Allotment*, New Holland, 2007

Foley, C., *Practical Allotment Gardening*,
New Holland, 2008

Harrison , J., *The Essential Allotment Guide*,
Right Way, 2009

Leendertz, L., *The Half Hour Allotment*,
Frances Lincoln, 2006

Liebreich, K.; Wagner, J.; Wendland, A.,
The Family Kitchen Garden, Frances Lincoln, 2009

Nicol, A.; Perrone, J., *The Allotment Keeper's Handbook*,
Atlantic Books, 2007

Poole, S., *The Allotment Chronicles: A Social History of Allotment Gardening*, Silver Link Publishing, 2006

Rand, M., *Close to the Veg: a Book of Allotment Tales*,
Marlin Press, 2005

Stewart, A., *The Earth Moved: On the Remarkable Achievements of Earthworms*, Algonquin Books, 2004

Stokes, G., *Teach Yourself Allotment Gardening*,
Teach Yourself, 2009

Wagland, P., *Practical Allotments*, Guild of
Master Craftsmen Publications, 2008

Your Allotment, Cassell Illustrated, 2007

Websites

www.allotments4all.co.uk
A Lively discussion forum enabling allotment holders to share thoughts and advice. Also includes an allotment 'wiki' providing lots of information.

www.allotments-uk.com
A directory of allotment sites to help you find, manage and get the best from a plot, including hints, tips, news and links.

www.allotment.org.uk
A website run by allotment expert John Harrison with advice, a diary page and links.

www.communitycompost.org
The Community Composting Network encourages small groups such as allotment holders to become involved in community composting and manage the organic waste they produce on site.

www.gardenorganic.org.uk
Garden Organic is Britain's national charity for organic growing, with advice and online leaflets.

www.gardenorganic.org.uk/hsl
Part of Garden Organic, the Heritage Seed Library aims to conserve and make available vegetable varieties that are not widely available, and offers advice, guidelines and an international focus.

www.jardins-familiaux.org
Jardins Familiaux is a European organization of allotment and leisure garden federations with more than three million leisure-gardener members.

www.kleingarten-bund.de
The German Leisure Garden Federation represents 19 regional organizations (Landesverbände) for Germany's 998,000 allotment gardens used by more than 4 million people.

www.nagtrust.org
National Allotment Gardens Trust is a charity promoting the benefits of allotments, with details on events such as National Allotment Week in the UK.

www.nsalg.org.uk
National Society of Allotment and Leisure Gardeners represents allotments and allotment gardens across Britain and offers advice, news and a 'frequently asked questions' page.

www.nvsuk.org.uk
National Vegetable Society is a charity promoting the improvement of vegetables targeted at growers who enter or want to enter competitions and shows.

www.rhs.org.uk
The Royal Horticultural Society is Britain's foremost gardening charity with excellent resources and a useful how-to-grow-your-own section.

www.sags.org.uk
The Scottish Allotments and Gardening Society promotes networking and campaigning on allotments and raising awareness of relevant planning issues.

www.soilassociation.org
The Soil Association is a UK environmental charity promoting sustainable growing and farming practices.

Index